ALCATRAZ

"Island of Many Mistakes"

Francis J. Clauss

BRIARCLIFF PRESS, INC.

Briarcliff Press, Inc.
Menlo Park, California

FOREWORD

Alcatraz is a small island in San Francisco Bay aptly described as "The Rock." In the two hundred years since the first Spanish explorers arrived in 1769, it has been:

- A natural sanctuary for thousands of pelicans and sea gulls, which inspired several of its earliest names, such as "Bird Island," "White Island" (because of its frosting of bird droppings), and "Isla de Alcatraces" (Spanish for Island of Pelicans).
- The site of the first lighthouse on the West Coast (1854).
- A fort for the United States Army (from 1859 to 1933). At the time of the Civil War, Alcatraz was the most heavily fortified site on the West Coast, and nervous San Franciscans looked to the soldiers stationed there to defend them against the Confederate raiders that never came.
- A military prison, which through the years was variously used to incarcerate soldiers guilty of going AWOL and other offenses, secessionists who plotted to capture San Francisco for the Confederate cause, Indian prisoners of war during the 1870s to 1890s, plus assorted enemy aliens, espionage agents, and POWs during World War I.
- A temporary lockup for San Francisco's prison population made "homeless" by the great earthquake of 1906.
- The notorious federal prison that housed "Scarface Al" Capone, "Machine Gun" Kelly, and many others of the nation's toughest criminals (1934 to 1963).
- The inspiration for a number of Hollywood movies, such as "Alcatraz Island" (1937, starring Ann Sheridan), "Birdman of Alcatraz" (1962, with Burt Lancaster as the birdman), and "Escape from Alcatraz" (1979, with Clint Eastwood).
- An Indian "war camp," captured in 1969 and occupied until 1971.
- A prime tourist attraction, since 1972 a part of the Golden Gate National Recreation Area.

This book provides a brief history of Alcatraz Island. The various books and articles that provided the material on which this brief history is based are identified in the section "Notes and References" at the end of this book. The author wishes to express his indebtedness to the following persons and organizations who were helpful in providing information, maps and photographs: Park Historian James P. Delgado, District Ranger Robert Kirby, Supervisory Park Technician Ruth Lawrence, and Archivist Vincent Piantanida, all of the

Golden Gate National Recreation Area; Mr. Wayne Wheeler, Assistant Chief of the Aids to Navigation Branch of the Twelfth Coast Guard District; Ms. Gladys Hansen, Archivist and Director of the San Francisco History Room at the San Francisco Public Library and her staff; the staff of the Bancroft Library of the University of California at Berkeley; and the staff of the California Historical Society in San Francisco. I am indebted to my colleague at De Anza College and expert on Russian history in California, Professor Nicholas Rokitiansky, for calling my attention to one of the island's early names. The photographs on the book's cover and on page 82 were provided through the courtesy of the Redwood Empire Association; credits for other photographs are given with the captions. On the production side, Mr. Richard Weismann of the My Word! word processing service bureau rendered the manuscript into finished text, Mr. Kenneth Moore prepared the camera-ready copy and provided artwork, and Mr. William Vecchio of Consolidated Publications assisted with suggestions and shepherded the work through its actual printing. Finally, the manuscript benefited from the sharp eyes and sense of style of a dear friend, Mrs. M. Nilson, and my wife, Mary Jean Clauss, both of whom offered many suggestions to improve its readability. My sincere thanks to all.

Francis J. Clauss
Menlo Park, California
April 1981

Table of Contents

Foreword iii

DISCOVERY AND NAMING 1

THE ROCK 3

THE BATTLESHIP IN THE BAY 5

FIRST LIGHTHOUSE ON THE WEST COAST 11

COMBINATION FORT AND MILITARY PRISON 15

NEW LIGHTHOUSE 25

MILITARY PRISON AND DISCIPLINARY BARRACKS 27

FEDERAL PENITENTIARY 35

INDIAN CAMP 55

ENJOYING ALCATRAZ TODAY 61

EPILOGUE 83

NOTES AND REFERENCES 85

NOTE TO VISITORS: Those using this book as a guide for visiting the island may find it useful to skip directly to the section beginning on page 61, which contains a description of the buildings in the sequence usually followed on the guided tours and maps of the island and the cellhouse.

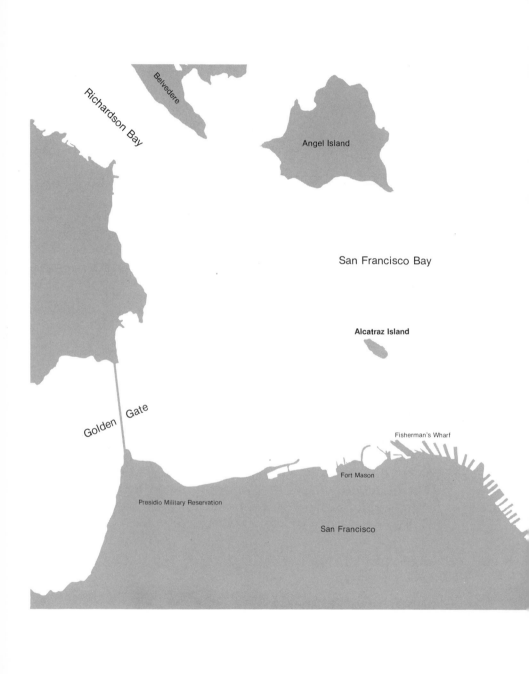

DISCOVERY AND NAMING

What is Alcatraz? Ask almost anyone and you'll be told that it's a former federal prison. As a one-time prison, Alcatraz is indeed an island of many mistakes—those of the thousand-plus convicts who served time there, some of whom added the final mistake of trying to escape.

But the prisoners' mistakes were neither the only ones nor the first. San Francisco's history as a city might have started many years earlier if it had not been for the mistakes of early Spanish explorers caused by Alcatraz. More mistakes were made when the island was named and as it was adapted to the uses of man. Some mistakes were tragic and others were simply humorous. For Alcatraz is above all a fascinating reminder of human fallibility.

* *

The mistakes began with the island's position in San Francisco Bay—-three miles inside the Golden Gate and directly behind it. To Spanish sea captains sailing some distance at sea to avoid shipwreck on California's rocky coast, it mistakenly appeared that the land mass extended unbroken from the Marin Headlands on the north to the San Francisco peninsula on the south, with Alcatraz Island visually closing the gap and hiding the opening. That effect fooled Spanish explorers for over two centuries. It hoodwinked even Cabrillo, the discoverer of San Diego and Monterey Bays, whose expedition in 1542 was searching for harbors along the coast. Cabrillo sailed right past the Golden Gate twice without spotting it or discovering the safe anchorage beyond. In similar fashion, Alcatraz helped fool the English privateer, Sir Francis Drake (in 1579), and the captains of countless Spanish galleons as they sailed home to Mexico with their treasures from China. Although every captain ached for a respite after crossing the Pacific Ocean and reaching the coast of northern California, not one perceived the gap in the shoreline at the Golden Gate or imagined the magnificent sanctuary that was so near.

It remained for a *land* expedition to discover San Francisco Bay and Alcatraz. This came about during the expedition led by Don Gaspar de Portola in 1769. The mistake here was that Portola was actually searching for another bay—the bay of Monterey, already discovered by Cabrillo, where Portola was directed to found a mission and presidio. Portola and his men hiked right past their goal without recognizing it. By the time they reached the San Francisco peninsula, they were tired and ready to admit they had come too far. While the chief scout reconnoitered, several hungry soldiers set out in search of food. Climbing to the top of Sweeney Ridge (a few miles south of today's Skyline

1

College), the hunters saw before them to the east the immense bay of San Francisco. It was a much better harbor than Monterey Bay. But orders from the Spanish crown were sacred, so Portola retraced his steps and the following June founded the mission and presidio at Monterey.

The Spanish did not forget their lucky discovery, and in succeeding years they explored the San Francisco Bay area thoroughly. Their chronicles for 1770 make the first mention of today's Alcatraz Island, then referred to simply as "a rock island." It was the smallest of the three islands they noted in the Bay, the other two being known today as Angel Island (the largest) and Yerba Buena Island.

Alcatraz first appeared on Spanish maps in 1775, but without a name. The omission persisted for the next half century, until an Englishman "lifted" its name from another island. The original Spanish name was *Isla de Alcatraces*, which means "Island of Pelicans." The name was coined by Juan Manuel de Ayala, the young Spanish naval lieutenant who made the first nautical survey of San Francisco Bay in 1775, one year before the founding of the mission and presidio at San Francisco. Ayala hit upon the name, as he reported it, "on account of the abundance of those birds (pelicans) that were on it." However, he was looking at another island, today's Yerba Buena Island, when he made that observation. On Ayala's map of 1775 and on all other maps of San Francisco Bay in the following decades, the name *Isla de Alcatraces* is given to what we know today as Yerba Buena Island, where the two sections of the San Francisco-Oakland Bay Bridge join. Today's Alcatraz Island appeared on the maps with no name at all, for the Spanish explorers thought it too insignificant.

The Spaniards' omission was unintentionally rectified by an Englishman, Frederic Beechey. Beechey was commander of the British exploring vessel *Blossom*, which first visited the area in 1826. On his map Beechey misplaced the name from one island to the other. And in his confusion he misspelled it as Alcatrazes. Beechey's mistake has been perpetuated on all subsequent maps of San Francisco Bay. Even his misspelling of the plural form endured until 1851, when the U. S. Coast Survey officially created the present singular version, "Alcatraz Island." Unofficially, the sailors of early whaleships and trading vessels gave the island several other names, most notably "Bird Island" and "White Island," the latter referring to the island's whitewashing by the droppings of generations of birds.

As for the pelicans that inspired the island's official name, one finds it difficult today to picture the thousands of pelicans that once flew over the Bay area. Man and DDT have taken their toll! But back in 1827 a visitor wrote that their number was so great on Alcatraz Island that "a rifle shot we fired across these feathered legions made them rise in a dense cloud with a noise like that of a hurricane."

Although there were many birds on the island, there were no people. Indians shunned it as the dwelling place of evil spirits. Through almost eighty years of Spanish and Mexican rule (1769 to 1848), no one ever dwelt there or used it for any purpose. Alcatraz Island was "strictly for the birds."

2

THE ROCK

An Army report of 1853 described Alcatraz Island as no more than "a mass of rock with a very thin crust of soil and of bird manure on the surface." Its nickname, "The Rock," has seemed appropriate for countless soldiers, prisoners, and others who have spent time there. For Alcatraz *is* a rock, and is just as barren and harsh as the term implies. Geologically it's a fine-grained and very compact type of sandstone with a bluish-green tinge of color. The fact that it's too soft and crumbly for building purposes may have saved Alcatraz from disappearing during San Francisco's building boom after the Gold Rush of 1849.

Except for a few tufts of grass, The Rock was utterly devoid of any vegetation until the 1860s, after it had become a U. S. fort. Soil was then brought from the mainland and scattered in pockets among the rocks to create gardens that helped soften the harshness for officers and their wives. It was necessary to bring water as well as soil, for the island has no springs or other sources of water of its own. Water for the early Army fort and later federal prison on Alcatraz Island had to be transported there by barge—first from Sausalito, which had a better supply of fresh water than early San Francisco, and later from the wharf at Fort Mason.

The Rock measures 1,700 feet long by 590 feet wide at its extremes and covers an area of only twelve acres. It does not spread out from a peaked summit to a broad base at its waterline, as does its neighbor Angel Island. Instead, Alcatraz rises abruptly to a mesa-like top that is 135 feet above water level. Its sides are precipitous and there are sheer drops of 75 feet into the water at several spots. With the exception of one or two places, its sides are so steep that a landing can be made only with the greatest difficulty.

There are heavy riptides about the island and currents range from 3 to 10 miles per hour. The tides that rush in and out through the Golden Gate are especially turbulent about Alcatraz. Through the ages they have eroded the island's flanks and left it as a spindle of rock that juts up from the Bay. The cold waters and swift currents have doomed many prisoners who attempted to swim from the island.

The Rock is cold and clammy and often shrouded in fog. Its location directly behind the Golden Gate exposes it to the full blast of the cold winds and fog that sweep in from the ocean almost every afternoon of the year.

When the weather is clear, Alcatraz Island enjoys a spectacular view of San Francisco, the Marin Headlands, Sausalito, Belvedere, Tiburon, and the cities of the East Bay. The Rock is closest to the city of San Francisco. The wharves along Embarcadero Street are only about one and a quarter miles distant, and sightseers peering at Alcatraz through the telescopes atop Telegraph

Hill are only slightly further away. The barreness and isolation of Alcatraz Island are in marked contrast to the magnificent scenery and pleasurable living that surround it. Tantalizingly close and yet so far out of reach, the attractions of San Francisco and the Bay area must have been a devilish psychological torture for any unfortunate detained on The Rock.

A GUN CREW AND ITS OFFICERS POSED IN THE ORDNANCE YARD IN FRONT OF THE OLD ARMY CITADEL. This photograph was taken shortly after the Civil War ended and shows the uniforms of that era. The officer in front wears a sash and carries his saber against his right shoulder. The top of the gardens can barely be seen between the front of the citadel and the stack of cannon balls behind the gun crew. (Bancroft Library)

THE BATTLESHIP IN THE BAY

Because of the way it looms suddenly out of the water, Alcatraz Island suggests the appearance of a battleship permanently anchored in defense of the Bay. In fact, within a few years after the war with Mexico had ended and California had been ceded to the United States, Alcatraz Island became the most heavily fortified site on the west coast and was nicknamed "The Battleship in the Bay."

Colonel John C. Fremont, who led his troops across the Bay from Sausalito and spiked the guns of the Mexican presidio in June of 1846, immediately recognized the importance of Alcatraz Island for defensive purposes. Early in 1847, while he was Military Governor of California (California did not become a state with a civil governor until three years later), Fremont succeeded "as the legal representative of the United States" in purchasing Alcatraz Island for the sum of $5,000.

The small civilian population of early San Francisco was very fearful of an attack by the English and French, who had been covetous rivals of Uncle Sam for control of the west coast. In response to San Francisco's entreaties to Washington for defensive fortifications, the Army's Corps of Topographic Engineers completed the first detailed survey of Alcatraz Island in May of 1847, and the U. S. Congress appointed a commission of Army and Navy officers to prepare plans for fortifying the harbor. This commission assembled in San Francisco in April of 1849, the opening year of California's Gold Rush. The enlisted men who came with the commission to do the actual surveying and to prepare the drawings dreamt the same dreams of fantastic wealth from the goldfields as the others who thronged to California that year, and many of them deserted. The officers decided to withdraw a safe distance from temptation to Honolulu, where they spent the winter developing their plans in the balmy climate of the Hawaiian Islands.

The commission returned to San Francisco with its plans in March of 1850. The plans took into account such vital data as the width of the opening through the Golden Gate (approximately one mile from shore to shore), the distance of Alcatraz Island from the Gate (approximately three miles), and the range and accuracy of the smooth-bore cannons of the day (an "annoying fire" at a distance of two miles, and a fire that would be "quite effective" at a mile and a half). The commissioners recommended two mainland forts on opposite sides of the Golden Gate and an island fort on Alcatraz. To reinforce this first line of defense, they proposed additional batteries of cannon on Angel Island, Yerba Buena Island, and along San Francisco's shoreline at what is now Fort Mason. They also selected Benicia for the storehouses and arsenals of the

Army, and Mare Island for a Navy yard. By executive order of President Millard Fillmore on November 6, 1850, these areas were reserved to the U. S. government for military reservations.

President Fillmore's directive did not automatically give the land to the government. Much of California belonged to Mexican rancheros whose property rights had been guaranteed by the terms of the peace treaty between the United States and Mexico (the Treaty of Guadalupe Hidalgo, which both governments signed on February 2, 1848). And although Fremont had reputedly paid $5,000 for Alcatraz Island on behalf of the United States, the legal documents to support the claim were questionable. Perhaps Fremont had simply "requisitioned" the island without payment, as had been done so often when Army troops needed horses, cattle, or supplies from the Mexican rancheros, or perhaps the man from whom Fremont allegedly purchased the island didn't really own it. Legal proceedings are seldom quick and simple, and hence it was not until November 7, 1856 that a formal document, officially signed and witnessed, transferred title to the United States. The official cost was "one dollar and other good and vaulable considerations." It was a bargain in 1856, for by that time the government had already invested almost a million dollars in the island's fortifications.

In 1851, five years before its title to Alcatraz was cleared, the U. S. began preparing detailed plans for the forts and batteries about San Francisco Bay. A board of engineering officers with this responsibility convened in Washington in October of 1851. Their plans were approved a year later by Jefferson Davis, who was then U. S. Secretary of War but in the following decade was to serve as the first president of the Confederate States of America with intimate knowledge of the fortifications of the Union Army. Actual construction of the fortifications on Alcatraz Island began towards the end of 1853.

Three open batteries were planned with cannons on barbette-type mounts, their muzzles pointing over parapets. The guns were described as 68-, 42-, and 28-pounders, which meant that they fired round iron balls weighing these amounts. By the spring of 1855 the first eight guns were mounted on the south battery, facing the city.

Work on the balance of the island's fortifications progressed. A large furnace was built for heating shot and cannonballs red-hot in order to set afire the wooden ships of an attacking force. Three bomb-proof powder magazines were cut into the solid rock of the island. The only sloping access to the island, on the southeast side, was blasted away to make landing there more difficult. Near the dock a strong guardhouse with a drawbridge and heavy gate controlled access to the fort. A massive three-story "citadel" or defensive battacks was constructed on the crest of the island. Next to the citadel was built an underground cistern that held enough water to supply 200 men for six months.

By 1859 the citadel was completed and 75 guns had been mounted. In brief ceremonies on December 30, 1859, Company H of the Third Artillery officially assumed command. The Army was to remain in command of the island for the next seventy-four years. Its troops considered their fort impregnable, but no enemy forces ever appeared to test their belief.

A FORMAL PORTRAIT OF GARRISON LIFE ON ALCATRAZ ISLAND IN THE 1870s. The stern-faced officers and their wives, along with a lovely young miss in a white dress and garden hat, are posed in the gardens across the front of the citadel. What appear at first to be high narrow windows are actually angled rifle slits, since the citadel was intended to be the last defense of the island's garrison. (Bancroft Library)

As civil war between the North and South grew imminent, the fortifications on Alcatraz Island were increased. By the end of 1860 the three batteries had a total of 91 cannons peering over their parapets. The first of the batteries, which mounted 35 cannons, commanded the Bay in the direction of the city. The second battery, with 16 guns, faced the Golden Gate and could fire point-blank at ships entering through that narrow opening. Both the first and second batteries provided cross-fire with the guns of Fort Point on the south side of the Gate. The third battery, with 40 guns, was on the north side of Alcatraz and faced Sausalito and Angel Island; it was intended to prevent enemy ships from running up the Bay to the Navy yard at Mare Island and the arsenal at Benicia. The ordnance included the largest cannons of the time — smooth-bore Columbiads with 12-inch muzzles that could hurl 120-pound balls a distance of three miles.

Construction was temporarily halted with the outbreak of the Civil War in 1861. By then Alcatraz was the most heavily fortified site on the west coast. In the spring of 1861 a detachment of engineer troops and three additional artillery companies joined the forces already there, raising the garrison's strength to eight officers and 361 enlisted men.

* *

Alcatraz's role as a prison began more or less by chance. Army posts had long maintained guardhouses for short-term lockups of soldiers guilty of insubordination, drunkenness, and other minor offenses. Long-term confinements for desertion and major offenses were a special problem for which the Army really had no established policies or prison system. In the summer of 1861 the commanding general of the Department of the Pacific was vexed by the growing number of prisoners in the guardhouse at the Presidio of San Francisco, and to improve military security he had them transferred to Alcatraz. On August 17, 1861 thirteen prisoners from the Presidio's guardhouse joined those already in the guardhouse on Alcatraz, and the island began its 102-year career as a prison.

The military offenders were soon joined by civilian prisoners. San Francisco's populace was then a conglomeration that the Gold Rush had attracted from all over the world, and although most were from America, the city's citizenry was as much divided as the rest of the country between Northern Unionists and Southern Secessionists. By a narrow margin California sided with the Northern Unionists. Early during the Civil War, Alcatraz began receiving civilians found guilty of disloyalty to the Union. An exciting moment came in March of 1863 when the schooner *Chapman,* secretly outfitted to operate as a Confederate raider against West Coast commerce, was seized in the harbor of San Francisco on the eve of going to sea. The armed crew of fifteen, led by the wonderfully-named Asbury Harpending, a Kentucky-born San Franciscan with a commission in his pocket signed by Jefferson Davis, was captured and taken to the military prison at Alcatraz. Among others who were incarcerated there for advocating the Confederate cause were a member of the state legislature and a former governor of California!

Although records for the civilians and military prisoners confined during the Civil War are not complete, it appears that the number of military prisoners alone averaged about fifteen during the first two years and there were forty-nine at war's end. The actual number of prisoners held at Alcatraz during the Civil War was never high, but the prison was so small that inmates had to sleep crowded together on the floor.

It was during this wartime period that several Confederate prisoners-of-war managed to row off the island and became the island's first escapees. They were not the last.

* *

With all the names that were bestowed so freely upon the island, it's surprising that the Army itself never properly named its fort there. Instead, the War Department always officially referred to the fort as "the Post at Alcatraz Island." An attempt at a proper baptism was made near the end of the Civil War. The commanding general of the Pacific forces proposed that the fort be named after the late Major General McPherson, but the War Department never even acknowledged the request. It would have been an appropriate name, for General James Birdseye McPherson had arrived at Alcatraz in 1857 as a second lieutenant to take charge of the fort's construction, and the citadel was completed under his supervision. (McPherson left for active service during the Civil War and rose rapidly in rank. He took command of the Army of Tennessee when Grant went east, and he was killed in the Atlanta campaign in 1864.)

In a letter written to a friend shortly after being posted to Alcatraz, McPherson lamented on the bleakness of his island assignment, but added: "San Francisco beats all the cities I have ever been in, in the way of Drinking Saloons, Billiard Tables, Cigar Stores, and idle men 'loafers' genteelly dressed." A century and a quarter later, the details have changed only slightly, and San Francisco's attractions persist as strongly as ever.

CREW OF A 15-INCH RODMAN CANNON STAGING A GUN DRILL, ABOUT 1870. In the foreground are two neat stacks of cannonballs, which frame the group of four men half-stooping to lift a cannonball for placing it into the cannon's muzzle. The officer in charge seems to be pointing towards an imaginary enemy ship sailing through the Golden Gate. The two men in front of the cannon's muzzle at the right are grabbing a long pole; at the other end, inside the muzzle, is a "swabber" for cleaning out the barrel after the last shot. The two men at the left have the powder box between them. The gunner behind the cannon's breech is holding his left thumb over the firing hole to prevent unburnt powder from igniting when the swabber is pushed into the barrel; he carries a pouch behind him that contains the primer for detonating the next powder charge. The gun is mounted on a "transverse carriage" that rotates about a center pintle for aiming. The manpower for aiming the gun will be provided by the four soldiers standing half at attention, who will push or pull the carriage to rotate it to the position directed by the gunner. San Francisco is in the background, with Telegraph Hill at the left. (Bancroft Library)

FIRST LIGHTHOUSE ON
THE WEST COAST

While San Francisco Bay ranks as one of the great harbors of the world, it would be a mistake to overlook the hazards that guard its entrance—contrary tides, shifting winds, periodic dense fogs, offshore rocks, and dangerous shoals. Ayala was the first to demonstrate the perils. In 1775, having completed his nautical survey of the Bay, as described earlier, Ayala left his safe anchorage at Angel Island and headed for the Gate. On his way out, he scraped his ship against the rocks at Lime Point and damaged its rudder. Ayala was not only the first European to sail through the Golden Gate but was also its first nautical mishap. His departure was delayed a week to repair the damage.

With the discovery of gold in California and the beginning of the Gold Rush in 1849, San Francisco became the goal of countless Argonauts jammed aboard an armada of ships. Many ships were barely seaworthy but were nevertheless pressed into service to reap quick profits for their owners. The ships were built of wood and their hulls were not divided by bulkheads, so that any sizeable hole caused by striking a rock, for example, meant quick flooding and sinking. California's coastline is notoriously rocky, and navigational aids to warn of its hazards were absent. As a result many Argonauts never reached port but died in shipwrecks along the coast.

In 1850, the year that California became a state, only the Atlantic and Gulf Coasts of the United States had lighthouses, and these were under the unlikely jurisdiction of the U. S. Treasury Department. It was not a satisfactory arrangement. To remedy the problems, Congress established on October 9, 1852 a nine-member Lighthouse Board composed of engineers, scientists, and military men to administer a civilian service that in time came to be known as the U. S. Lighthouse Service. The first headquarters of the U. S. Lighthouse Service were at San Francisco, and its first major project was the construction of a chain of lighthouses along California's shoreline. The first was at Alcatraz Island, the very first lighthouse on the Pacific Coast.

The basic plan of all California lighthouses was a short tower with a Cape Cod-style cottage for the keeper and his family. The one on Alcatraz Island had two stories and a basement, with a tower that ran in the center up through the roof and lifted the oil lantern 160 feet above the waters of the Bay. The lantern was reached by a spiral staircase placed a few feet from the keeper's bedroom.

The original Alcatraz lighthouse was located at the southeast end of the island's high plateau (a bit to the west of the present lighthouse, which replaced it in 1909). Construction began on December 15, 1852 and the structure was completed early the following year. It was painted white with black trim, but

ORIGINAL ALCATRAZ LIGHTHOUSE. This lighthouse was placed into service on June 1, 1854 and was the first lighthouse on the Pacific Coast. The portly lightkeeper with walrus-type mustache stands near the foot of the entrance stairs, and his assistant is on the balcony that circles the lantern and lens. The sign near the window at the left indicates that the lighthouse station was also the island's post office. In the right background is the Army citadel, with several water tanks visible on its roof. (San Francisco Public Library)

for the next year and a half the new lighthouse was conspicuous only during the daytime—for its lens had not yet arrived!

The lens had been ordered from France. It was a third-order Fresnel lens, built at a cost of $3,800 and representative of the best optical technology of the day. Even after it reached San Francisco late in 1853, its installation was further delayed because of a lack of funds. Finally, on June 1, 1854 Lightkeeper Michael Cassin lit the wick of the lantern, and the first lighthouse on the west coast of the United States began operating. It provided a fixed (i.e., non-flashing) white light that was visible for 14 miles at sea, or about halfway to the Farallone Islands.

Perhaps it would be more correct to say that the light was visible at sea only when there was no fog. For another mistake was discovered—the lighthouse designers from the East had forgotten about California's coastal fogs, which frequently blotted out the lighthouse's rays. Therefore, acting on the rationale that "if they can't see you, maybe they can hear you," the Lighthouse Service decreed fog bells.

The first fog bell was added in 1856 at the south end of the island. It was an awkward expedient—simply a large bell that was struck by hand with a hammer. The job sounds ridiculously easy, but pounding a bell at short, fixed intervals in a dense fog gets tedious when the fog persists for hour after hour. Besides, if the bell is loud enough for a ship to hear at some distance, how much louder it must ring in the ears of the bell-ringer. The lighthouse keeper soon found the job unbearable and was repeatedly absent from his post, drowning his sorrow in San Francisco's saloons. Both he and the fog bell were soon replaced—the keeper by a more reliable person, and the hand-rung bell by one with a clockwork mechanism that struck the bell automatically. Once wound by raising a weight to its highest position, the clockwork mechanism would strike the bell at prescribed intervals for the next four hours, after which the weight had to be cranked back up. The new arrangement proved so successful that it remained in service until 1883, when it was replaced by a similar mechanism and a larger bell. In 1900 a second fog bell was located at the north end of the island.

By the turn of the century, San Francisco had grown to such a metropolis that sailors were making another type of mistake—they were confusing the old, fixed light on Alcatraz Island with the bright lights of the city. For that reason, in 1902 a new "bulls-eye" type of flashing lens replaced the old one. This gave the Alcatraz lighthouse a fourth-order light with a revolving lens that flashed white every 15 seconds.

VIEW OF ALCATRAZ ISLAND FROM THE NORTHEAST, ABOUT 1900.
Only a few of the buildings in this photograph remain today. The large
building on the plateau at the top center (with the water storage tanks
on its roof) is the old Army citadel, completed in 1859; this site is now
occupied by the prison cellhouse, built in 1909-1912. Immediately to
the south is the original lighthouse, which began service in 1854 and
was replaced by a taller one in 1909. The three residences on the cliff-
side to the east of the lighthouse are officers' quarters, built in
1880-1881; the largest one (in the middle of the row) was the commanding officer's home. The building at the south end of "officers'
row" is the post administrative headquarters, built in 1886; this building was replaced in the early 1900s by a larger home for the commandant, which became the home of Warden Johnston when the island
became a federal penitentiary in 1934. The collection of wooden frame
buidings on the leveled section at the south end (just below the headquarters building) is a temporary prison, constructed in 1900 to house
the overflow of military prisoners returned from the Philippines. Behind
the boat at the dock is the brick cannon casemate, begun in 1865 as
the foundation for permanent barracks for the enlisted men; on top of
these foundations can be seen a rather ugly temporary wooden barracks, constructed in the late 1800s and replaced in 1905 by the
concrete-block barracks that visitors see today. Along the wharf to the
south are quartermaster's offices and storehouses. To the north of the
barracks are the old guardhouse and sallyport, which still remain, and
the island's original prison building, which was demolished in the
1900s. (Bancroft Library)

COMBINATION FORT AND
MILITARY PRISON

Most wars are accompanied by such advances in technology that previous methods of warfare are made obsolete. So it was with the Civil War, which ended in 1865. Smooth-bore cannons firing round cannonballs with poor accuracy were superseded by rifled cannons that fired pointed projectiles and were orders of magnitude more accurate and destructive. Fortress walls that could have withstood a month-long siege from smooth-bore cannons could now be breached in hours. Wooden ships were replaced by ironclad monitors that could face with impunity the concentrated fire from the forts. The Army's "Post at Alcatraz Island" was obsolete even before it was completed. As the importance of its guns declined, that of its prison cells increased, and the Army decreed a new role for Alcatraz. Beginning officially in 1868, the fort was to combine its defensive role with that of a prison for long-term military offenders and incorrigibles.

As far as its continued defensive role was concerned, the plans for the island's fortifications were revised in the mid-years of the Civil War to strengthen the batteries with thicker earth embankments before the gun platforms. Other projects included placing "additional guns on the northeastern side of the island, additional permanent barracks, enlargements of the military prison, permanent storehouses, and improved hospital facilities." When new guns were promised which were larger than any previously mounted, the wharf had to be rebuilt to make it strong enough for unloading the heavier cannons. The new guns were the first 15-inch Rodman cannons on the Pacific coast, and their mounting at Alcatraz on July 20, 1864 called for great celebration. The merriment was marred by the deaths of two enlisted men who, in a state of intoxication brought on by the liquor provided for the celebration, tumbled off a 50-foot embankment.

With the increased size of the garrison on Alcatraz during the Civil War, the need for permanent barracks became more pressing. Plans were proposed towards the end of 1864 for a barracks that would house 800 men, along with provisions for four months, kitchens and mess halls, a wartime supply of ordnance stores, and a powder magazine. The building was to be a bombproof masonry structure. Its two lower floors were to provide casemates for mounting cannons, and the upper floors were to be quarters for enlisted men. Its location was on the east side of the island, hugging the side of the cliff just behind the wharf. This location took advantage of the island's plateau, which hid the barracks below the line of sight of enemy ships approaching from the west. Plans were finally approved and excavations began in the spring of 1865.

By January of 1867, with only the two lower tiers of the gun casemates completed, work was suspended to redesign the structure to withstand the new, heavier weapons. The enlisted men's "home" would not be completed until 1905. In the meantime a new Board of Engineers convened early in 1867, and in the spring of the following year they issued a revised master plan for the defense of San Francisco Bay. By then Alcatraz had 103 guns mounted. Nevertheless, the Board found that Alcatraz's defenses were completely unsatisfactory and recommended a wholesale revamping. The Engineers' report pointed out that a basic mistake had been made in the original design of the gun batteries. "The great difficulty is that the whole island is a mass of rock," their report observed, years after "The Rock" had become a common nickname among enlisted men, "and rising as it does immediately behind the guns, it is to be greatly feared that the batteries would be so insecure from splinters of stone that the gunners could not serve their guns." Remedies to correct the problems posed by the steep slopes of loose friable rock in the rear of the batteries progressed slowly and only minimal improvements were made in the fortifications during the late 1800s, as the U. S. Congress' annual appropriations were small.

* *

The Army's "Post at Alcatraz Island" continued its dual role as a military prison and part of the defensive network of San Francisco Bay for many years after the Civil War. Other important forts and batteries were Fort Point (on the south side of the Golden Gate), Camp Reynolds (on the west side of Angel Island), Lime Point Bluff (on the north side of the Golden Gate, later Fort Baker), Yerba Buena Island, and Rincon Point. The military activities of these Army posts helped make life interesting for local civilians. In addition to the theater, opera, restaurants, and the rowdy life of the Barbary Coast, San Franciscans were entertained by the parades, band concerts, and maneuvers staged by the military, who were a large part of the city's social scene in the late 1800s. The cannoneers of Alcatraz participated in one of these events—the great naval and artillery display celebrating the first centennial anniversary of our nation's independence on July 4, 1876. The highlight of the day's festivities was to be a bombardment between the gun batteries at the different locations, which would be climaxed by their sinking a target ship anchored in the Bay.

The show turned into a great flop! After hours of firing, not a single cannon ball hit the mark. Embarrassed officers finally directed a small boat to approach from behind and set fire to the target ship, hoping that the maneuver would go unnoticed and that spectators on shore would believe the gunners had finally managed to score. The deception fooled no one. An historian, writing a few months later, summed up the event: "Although the natural advantages for a means of defense are superior, this naval engagement proved beyond doubt that San Francisco's defensive ability, so far as relates to the engines of war and their manipulators, is not great. A single one of the more recently constructed iron-clad war vessels could steam up the channel of the harbor, and open a broadside fire in the heart of the city, without fear of being disabled by a shot

16

MAIN ROAD FROM THE DOCK TO THE MILITARY PRISON, 1890-1914. In the center is the old guardhouse and sallyport, with the chapel on top and the overseer's squad room over the chapel. At the left is the old fortification wall with the paint shop just visible above. On the right is the blacksmith shop. (Golden Gate National Recreation Area)

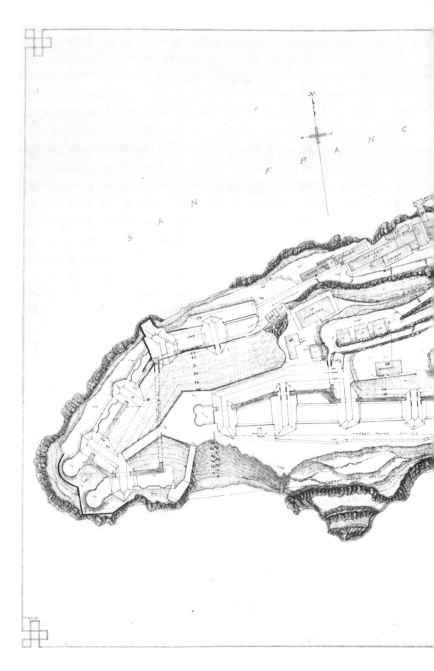

MAP OF 1894. This map shows the location of the original Army Citadel, completed in 1859, with gardens and a tennis court between the
Citadel and the lighthouse. (The Citadel was demolished in 1909 to
make room for the present prison cellhouse.) This map also shows the
series of massive gun batteries along the west side and at the north
and south ends. (Golden Gate National Recreation Area)

18

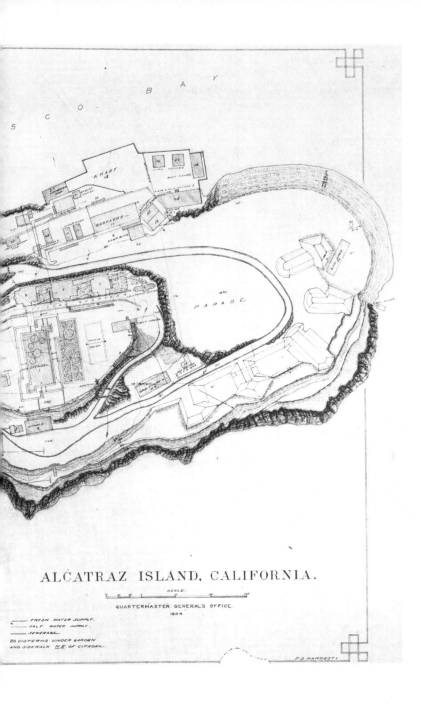

ALCATRAZ ISLAND, CALIFORNIA.

SCALE.

QUARTERMASTER GENERAL'S OFFICE.
1894

FRESH WATER SUPPLY.
SALT WATER SUPPLY.
SEWERAGE.
20 CISTERNS UNDER GARDEN
AND SIDEWALK N.E. OF CITADEL.

F.S. HARDESTY.

from our most formidable batteries. Big guns, and well-drilled gunners, are wanting."

Least concerned about San Francisco's defenses on that centennial day were several of the military prisoners on Alcatraz. During the distractions provided by the target practice, they had managed to break into the reception room of the commanding officer, where a great quantity of "distilled spirits" had been set out for the day's distinguished guests. The happy imbibers were apprehended and sent back to their cells. Still, they had found better reason to celebrate than any of the island's officers.

* *

ALCATRAZ FROM THE SOUTHEAST, ABOUT 1912. The new light-house and the prison cellhouse behind it appear complete. The group of wooden frame buildings on the level below are a temporary prison, built in 1900 and demolished a few years after this photograh was taken. The two-story wooden building to the left of the flagpole was the prison office. The small building immediately to the left of the prison office and on the edge of the cliff houses a fog bell; behind it is a slender tower that houses a dropping weight to actuate a hammer that strikes the bell at prescribed intervals. Behind the flagpole can be seen the top of the enlisted men's barracks, completed in 1905. The calibrated dial at water level is a tide gauge. (Twelfth Coast Guard District)

The years between the end of the Civil War and the beginning of the Spanish-American War in 1898 were those of our nation's westward expansion. To the Army's career officers and enlisted men went the job of protecting the settlers and subduing the native Americans. Military actions consisted of a series of wars against the Indians. Beginning in the 1870s, the military prison at Alcatraz started receiving redskin prisoners-of-war from territories as far north as Alaska and as far south as the Mexican border. The bitter war against the Modoc Indians in northern California, so costly and tragic in its outcome, ended in the capture of four of their leaders. The chief and one other were executed, and the other two Modocs were sent as prisoners to Alcatraz in October of 1873. One died in prison the following year, and the other was released two years later. The largest single contingent of Indian prisoners sent to Alcatraz was a group of nineteen Hopi braves from Arizona; they came in January of 1895 and returned to their reservation in September of the same year.

Not all the prisoners on Alcatraz were Indians. Most were military offenders from the Army itself. These were of two types: general prisoners who had sentences to serve but were still in the Army, and military convicts who had been court martialed for such crimes as desertion. Most of these military prisoners during the 1870s were young men in their twenties and thirties, and their average confinement was about five years. For those who gave trouble, punishments were severe. Although flogging had been discontinued by this time, wearing a 12-pound ball and chain at hard labor was still part of the punishment for misbehavers. Branding with hot irons had also been stopped, but each deserter or thief had the appropriate letter, D or T, tatooed on his hip. Solitary confinement in a black hole and a diet of bread and water was the fate of the most hardened.

Towards the end of the Civil War there had generally been between ten and twenty soldiers confined in the military prison on Alcatraz, and the engineering officer proposed to use them in such work as "breaking stones" in order to advance the work on the fortifications and to stretch his meager budget. The first cautious trials were successful and the size of the convict work force was gradually increased. It numbered between thirty and fifty prisoners early in 1869, and between eighty and one hundred by the fall of 1870. In addition to "rock bustin'," prisoners provided free labor for excavating foundations, dismounting the older cannons, and tearing-out decayed wooden gun platforms that were to be replaced with stone ones. Prisoners who "earned good reputations as laborers" had their sentences shortened in order to help motivate their toils. One of the major changes made by the prisoners' pick-and-shovel brigade to the island's appearance, which is still visible today, was the cutting-down and leveling of the southeast end of the island in 1875. This was done to provide a site for permanent quarters and a parade ground. Instead, it was to furnish the site for a temporary prison twenty-five years later.

The use of military prisoners for heavy construction work continued at Alcatraz and other Army posts for many years. The work was especially hard and dismal on The Rock, so that the island very early began to take on a dreaded reputation. A soldier stationed in the Philippine Islands in 1898, during the

Spanish-American War, wrote to his mother: "When a man is given one or two years or a term of years, it means hard labor in a military prison in the U. S., probably Alcatraz. The one who was given one year had his sentence read out the day I was Corp. of Guard, and of the curses I ever heard, his was the worst."

Although it is hardly noted for a balmy climate, Alcatraz Island took on the unlikely role of "health resort" during the Spanish-American War and the Philippine Insurrection that continued until 1902. For the first time in its history, the U. S. Army had troops fighting on hot, humid battlefields that exposed them to malaria and other tropical diseases. Besides healthy soldiers returning home, the ships from the Philippines carried two types of customers for Alcatraz—some were offenders in the brig destined for hard labor and others were soldiers who were ill. The sick troops were first diagnosed at the General Hospital at the Presidio of San Francisco, where they were formed into "Convalescent Companies" and shipped either to Alcatraz or Angel Island for isolation and recuperation.

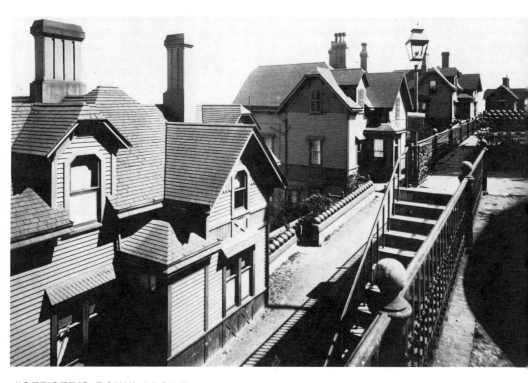

"OFFICER'S ROW," ABOUT 1893. These three homes for officers of the Army's military prison were built in 1880-1881 along the southeast edge of the upper plateau. The largest (between the other two) was for the commanding officer. At the far end of "officers' row" is the administrative headquarters for the Army's garrison. Note the lamp, the ornamented iron fence and gate, and the neat stack of cannonballs. (Golden Gate National Recreation Area)

Alcatraz's role as a military prison expanded as the number of convicted personnel returned from the Philippine Islands grew. During the summer of 1899 the average number of military prisoners had been only twenty-five, but by April of 1900 it had jumped to 441! The size of the garrison doubled at the same time, and facilities were strained to the limit. A new temporary prison was constructed at the southeast end of the island, the area that had been leveled earlier for a parade ground. The next ten years saw an outburst of building activity on the island. In 1905 the enlisted men, who had been living in a succession of temporary wooden-frame buildings for most of the forty-five years that the island had been garrisoned, were finally rewarded with the completion of their own permanent barracks, which had been started in 1865. The ugly temporary structure that had been built on top of the masonry casemates along the cliff above the wharf area was torn down and replaced by a three-story structure of concrete block. The cost of these barracks was kept remarkably low (only $20,000) by using prison labor to manufacture the hollow concrete blocks and to do most of the structural work.

* *

Many prisoners tried to escape from Alcatraz in the late 1800s and a surprisingly large number were successful. In May of 1878 two military prisoners were reported to have escaped in a small boat; more escaped in 1884 on a boat they had stolen from the Engineering Department; another prisoner escaped by unspecified means in December of 1892; and three more prisoners were reported to have escaped in a small boat in August of 1898.

While boats were the favored means for leaving the island, prisoners resorted to an amazing variety of substitutes when they could not acquire one. Four prisoners in 1906, for example, stole a butter vat from the post bakery and floated off the island in it, only to be forced back by the wind and the tide. A short time later three prisoners, inspired perhaps by the nursery rhyme of "Rub-a-dub-dub, three men in a tub," put to sea in a dough kneading trough and met the same fate as the butter-vat sailors. A lone convict floated off the island on a log, but he had the misfortune to be hit by a ferry; the crew of the ferry hauled him out of the Bay's icy waters and returned him to Alcatraz.

Shortly after the turn of the century, four prisoners managed to escape by a remarkably clever means. It was so clever they were not even missed, and their escape might have gone undetected except for a newspaper reporter who had heard a rumor of an escape. "Yes, it was true that four prisoners had left the island," admitted Major Paxton, the commanding officer of the prison, "but all four had been pardoned." Asked by the reporter if the pardons were in order, Major Paxton replied testily, "Certainly. Signed by the Adjutant General in Washington, the Judge Advocate of the Department of California, and the Assistant Adjutant General of the Department of California. All according to regulations." It all appeared fine, except that in answer to a cable from the reporter to officials in Washington came word that they had issued no pardons to anyone at Alcatraz in the past four months!

Under questioning, some prisoners broke down and supplied information for piecing together what had happened. One prisoner who worked in the print shop had printed four War Department letterheads on blank Alcatraz stationery, and another who worked in the mail room and had handled many pardons was able to fill in the forms correctly and forge the proper signatures. A guard was bribed to take the bogus pardons to San Francisco and mail them back to Alcatraz. Since they arrived at Alcatraz by regular mail, there was simply no reason for anyone to doubt their authenticity. The prisoners were pardoned and escorted off the island by the jailers themselves! Unfortunately, the secret was too good to keep, and three of the escapees were arrested two days later by military police who found them in a San Francisco tavern, blind drunk and boasting of their escape. The fourth, however, got away for keeps and was never heard of again.

* *

Early in the morning of April 18, 1906, San Francisco was wracked by a violent earthquake. Buildings tumbled and fires started that blazed continuously for the next three days and left the city utterly devastated. The structures on Alcatraz Island survived with little damage, a tribute both to the Army's construction methods and to the solid foundation provided by The Rock.

The new jailhouse was among the buildings destroyed in San Francisco. It was packed with 150 prisoners, most of them asleep when the earthquake struck. With masonry falling about them, the prisoners alternately screamed, cried, prayed, and cursed. An hour passed before a judge arrived to tell them there had been an earthquake and they were to be moved to another lockup. Those guilty of petty offenses were released, and the others were turned over to Army troops from the Presidio and taken to the old city jail on Broadway. However, as the fire was soon closing in about that jail, the prisoners had to be moved again almost immediately, and they were marched to the wharves and placed on a steamer that took them to the state prison at San Quentin. The warden refused to accept them, however, because they were Federal prisoners in charge of Army troops!

The steamer returned with its cargo of prisoners to San Francisco. The city was ablaze, and as the steamer approached the wharf, the captain saw the mobs of people awaiting him there, desperate with terror and screaming to be let aboard to escape the flames. The captain decided not to land, and instead he turned around and headed for Alcatraz. There the jailbirds were finally accepted and allowed to double up in the cells of the military prison. As one of them later put it, "I've never been so glad to see any place in my life as that damned Rock."

By April 21st almost two hundred prisoners had been moved from shore jails to Alcatraz, and most of them were happy to be there. A week later they had all been sent back to their respective hoosegows, and Alcatraz resumed its role as a fort and military prison.

NEW LIGHTHOUSE

San Francisco's earthquake of 1906 did only minor damage to the lighthouse on Alcatraz Island. But soon other problems arose—literally. The Lighthouse Service shared the island with the Army, and as the military fortifications and prison facilities grew in size and number, there was danger that they would soon overshadow the lighthouse and hide its light. To be dwarfed by one's neighbors is, of course, a ridiculous situation for any respectable lighthouse.

Matters came to a head when the Army announced it would convert its post exclusively to a military prison, as described in the next section. As part of that conversion the Army planned to erect a large cellhouse on the site of the old citadel, just to the north of the old lighthouse. To keep from being topped, the engineers of the Lighthouse Service designed a new tower for the light and a new dewelling for the keeper. These were located just to the east of the original lighthouse, and on December 1, 1909 their construction was completed and the new light went into service. The new tower was (and still is) an octagonal shaft of reinforced concrete rising 84 feet above the island itself, which puts the light more than 200 feet above the water. The lantern was reached by a spiral stairway of iron that reached to the lamp cleaning room and from there by a vertical ladder. The bulls-eye lens was transferred from the old lighthouse to the new, and the first lighthouse on the west coast was phased out after fifty-five years of service.

The new lighthouse was converted to automatic operation in November of 1963. Some years earlier the fog bells located at opposite ends of the island were replaced by fog horns.

"EXECUTIVE HILL," ABOUT 1930. In this view of the southeast end of the island, the lighthouse tower and the lightkeeper's home is in the center. The home of the commandant of the Army's prison is at the right; this became Warden Johnston's residence in 1934, when the old military prison became a federal penitentiary. Part of the prison cellhouse can be seen behind the lighthouse. The buildings on the hillside at the left are quarters for married soldiers. In the foreground is the parade ground, with end of a tennis court backstop at the right. (San Francisco Public Library)

MILITARY PRISON AND
DISCIPLINARY BARRACKS

A year after San Francisco's great earthquake and fire of 1906, the Army decided to discontinue its use of Alcatraz Island for defensive fortifications and to convert it solely to a military prison. Thus, in June of 1907, the Army's "Post at Alcatraz Island" was officially redesignated the "Pacific Branch, U. S. Military Prison." The four infantry companies that had served as the island's regular garrison left. They were replaced by the newly formed Third and Fourth Companies of the U. S. Military Guard, who took charge of the 285 prisoners then in confinement. Plans were developed to upgrade the facilities. The major element of these plans was the construction of a new permanent cellhouse to replace the temporary wooden structure that had been built in 1900 on the parade grounds at the southeast end of the island.

The 50-year old Citadel that had dominated the south end of the island's high plateau was demolished in 1909 to make way for the new cellhouse. The sum of $250,000 was allocated for the new cellhouse, and most of that was spent on materials. The bulk of the labor for building the cellhouse was provided by the military prisoners who were to occupy it. The first prisoners moved into their new "home" on February 6, 1912. The new cellhouse was built to hold 600 inmates, one to a cell. The most it ever actually held was 553, during its first month of use. For the next five years its average population varied between 359 and 469 prisoners. Some of these were enemy agents imprisoned during World War I.

The rules and regulations for the treatment of military prisoners included the following:

> On admission each convict was minutely searched and deprived of all his possessions except clothing.

> He then took a bath and was issued prison dress. His hair was cut short and he had to shave off any beard or mustache; however, during his last month of confinement he was allowed to grow a beard again, if he wished.

> A number was assigned to him, by which he was known during his prison term. Personal names were not used.

> For good conduct, a convict could earn an abatement of five days for each month of his first year of sentence and ten days per month for time over that. Earned abatement could be forefeited by misconduct.

> Prisoners received a wholesome and sufficient ration. Those in solitary confinement received 18 ounces of bread a day and as much water as they desired.

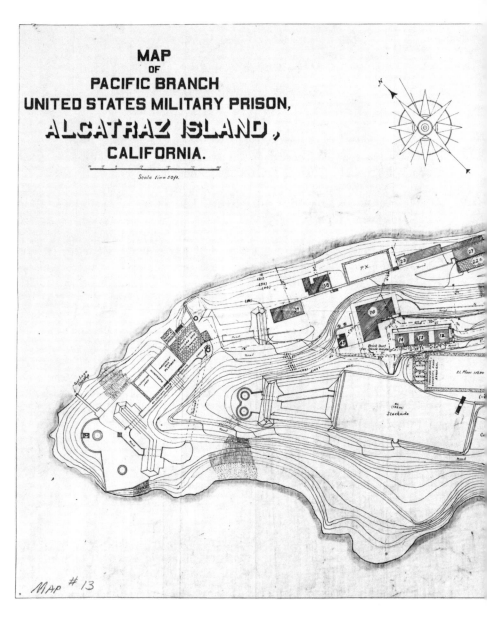

MAP
OF
PACIFIC BRANCH
UNITED STATES MILITARY PRISON,
ALCATRAZ ISLAND,
CALIFORNIA.

Scale 1in = 50ft.

MAP #13

MAP OF NOVEMBER 1910. The old Army Citadel has been replaced by the current prison cellhouse, which was constructed between 1909 and 1912. The collection of buildings on the parade ground at the southeast end of the island (numbered 11, 50 to 53, and 60 to 63) are temporary wooden buildings that comprised the military prison built at the turn of the century, following the Spanish-American War of 1898. These buildings were demolished after the permanent cellhouse was completed. (Golden Gate National Recreation Area)

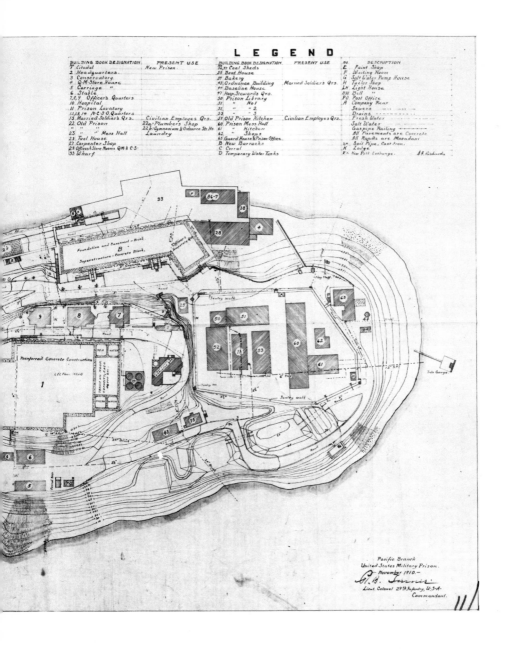

LEGEND

BUILDING BOOK DESIGNATION	PRESENT USE	BUILDING BOOK DESIGNATION	PRESENT USE		DESCRIPTION
1 Citadel	New Prison	34,35 Coal Sheds		E	Paint Shop
2 Headquarters		38 Boat House		F	Waiting Room
3 Conservatory		39 Bakery		G	Salt Water Pump House
4 Q.M. Store House		43 Ordnance Building	Married Soldiers Qrs.	H	Tailor Shop
5 Carriage "		44 Baseline House		I	Light House
6 Stable		47 Hosp. Stewards Qrs.		LH	Bell "
7,8,9 Officer's Quarters		50 Prison Library		P.O.	Post Office
10 Hospital		51 " No.1		R	Company Rear
11 Prison Lavatory		52 " - 2			Sewers
12,13,14 N.C.S.O. Quarters		53 " - 3			Drains
15 Married Soldiers Qrs.	Civilian Employes Qrs.	59 Old Prison Kitchen	Civilian Employes Qrs.		Fresh Water
22 Old Prison		60 Prison Mess Hall			Salt Water
" "	22a Plumber's Shop	61 " Kitchen			Gaspipe Railing
23 " " Mess Hall	22b Gymnasium & Ordnance Ste Ho.	62 " Shops			All Pavements are Concrete
25 Tool House	Laundry	63 Guard House & Prison Office.			All Roads are Macadam
27 Carpenter Shop		B New Barracks			Soil Pipe, Cast Iron.
28 Offices & Store Rooms Q.M. & C.S.		C Corral		K	Lodge
33 Wharf		D Temporary Water Tanks		P.X.	New Post Exchange.

Pacific Branch
United States Military Prison.
November 1910.

Lieut. Colonel 29th Infantry, U.S.A.
Commandant.

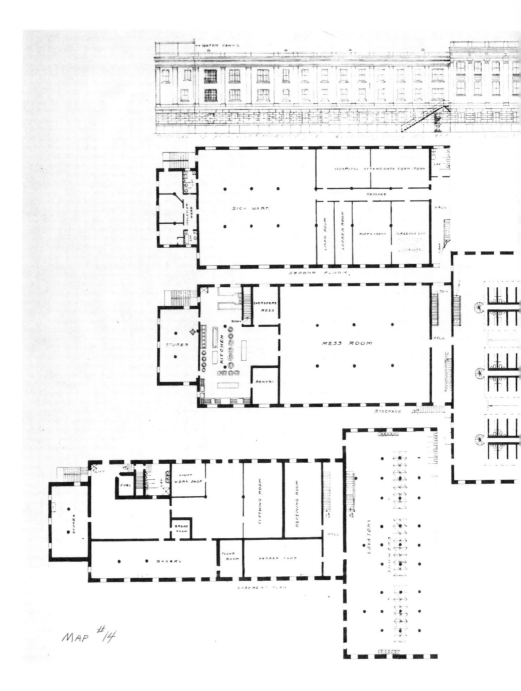

MAP #14

PLAN AND ELEVATIONS OF PRISON CELLHOUSE. (Golden Gate
National Recreation Area)

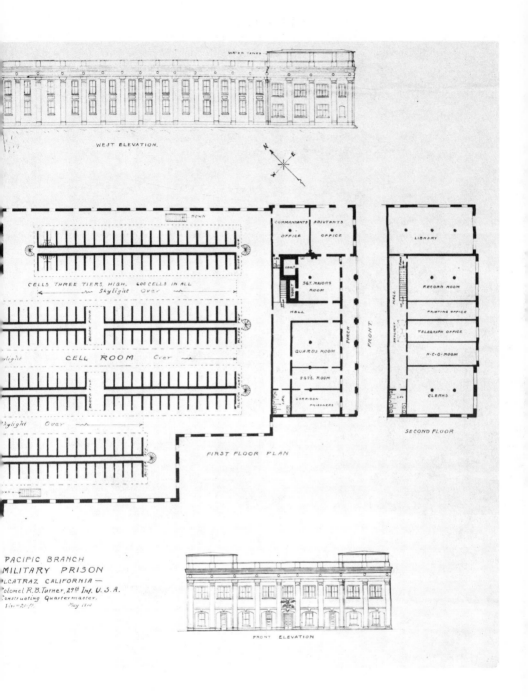

WEST ELEVATION.

CELLS THREE TIERS HIGH, 600 CELLS IN ALL
Skylight Over

CELL ROOM Over

Skylight Over

FIRST FLOOR PLAN

DOWN

COMMANDANTS OFFICE   ADJUTANTS OFFICE

VAULT

VAULT   SGT. MAJORS ROOM

HALL

GUARDS ROOM

SGTS. ROOM

GARRISON PRISONERS

PORCH

FRONT

LIBRARY

RECORD ROOM

PRINTING OFFICE

TELEGRAPH OFFICE

N.C.O. ROOM

CLERKS

HALL

SKYLIGHT

SECOND FLOOR

PACIFIC BRANCH
MILITARY PRISON
ALCATRAZ CALIFORNIA —
Colonel R.B. Turner, 29th Inf. U.S.A.
Constructing Quartermaster.
1in = 20 ft.   May 1910

FRONT ELEVATION

31

Convicts were kept at hard labor six days a week and were allowed time off on seven national holidays. The commandant could suspend labor during unusual weather to protect the health of prisoners. They engaged in every kind of police, maintenance, and construction activity, as well as clothing manufacture and rock breaking, not only on Alcatraz but at other posts around San Francisco Bay. (Many were used in the construction of the East Garrison at Angel Island.)

Every cell was inspected daily for cleanliness, contraband articles, or escape attempts. Weekly inspections of the convicts and the prison were also held.

LANDING DOCK AND LIVING QUARTERS FOR MARRIED GUARDS AND FAMILIES IN 1936. This large concrete-block building was formerly the barracks for enlisted soldiers; its foundations were begun in 1865, but the permanent barracks shown here were not completed until forty years later. The two-story wooden frame building with attic (behind the "CABLE CROSSING" sign) is the old quartermaster's storehouse. The lighthouse and warden's home are at the upper left. (San Francisco Public Library)

Convicts who violated the rules were disciplined. Punishments might be merely a reprimand or the deprivation of a meal. Severe infractions resulted in solitary confinement for fourteen days on bread and water, and some prisoners in solitary confinement were handcuffed to their cell doors as additional punishment. Convicts who attempted to escape lost all earned good-conduct time and had to serve their full sentences. Upon release from the prison, a soldier received a $10 suit of clothes, $5 in cash, and transportation back to his place of enlistment.

To keep the offenders busy and make their time useful, the military prison operated a fully-equipped furniture factory that turned out excellent furniture for Army posts. There was also a shoe factory. These were housed in the shops built at the north end of the island. And finally, what was most surprising on an island that had no water supply of its own, the Army established a laundry for washing the clothes of personnel from nearby military posts.

A power plant for supplying electricity and steam was completed in 1912 at the northeast end of the island over the site of an old gun battery. An officers' club was built along the seawall on the east side of the island (about midway between the old guardhouse and the new power plant) in 1912, and bowling alleys and a gymnasium were added later. (This officers' club was destroyed during the Indian occupation in 1971; visitors today can see only its ruins.)

By 1913 the Army fretted that its image was being tarnished by its conspicuous prison. More and more San Franciscans began asking questions about what was going on in the front yard of their city. In a wordy report to Congress, the Army's Judge Advocate General lamented: "[Alcatraz] lies directly in the path of commerce, and, surmounted as it is with the rather conspicuous new prison building, is perhaps more prominent in the view of the incoming passenger and more the subject of his inquiry and that of residents and visitors generally than any other object in the harbor. The answer they receive, that it is a prison for the confinement of our military defenders, gives an impression of the character of our enlisted personnel and of the discipline of our Army which is unfair and unjust to the service."

The Army pondered the problem, and in the interests of public relations they decided their military prison had to go—well, sort of. In a typical bit of Army wizardry, the "prison" was made to disappear into thin air simply by changing its name to "disciplinary barracks." More exactly, the military prison at Alcatraz was officially redesignated on March 4, 1915 as the "Pacific Branch, United States Disciplinary Barracks." To be fair, the Army did pack the more serious offenders off to federal penitentiaries and then set about to rehabilitate the more subdued wrongdoers that were left.

Not all of those who remained were content to stay on the island, and several escapes were attempted on improvised rafts. On Thanksgiving Day of 1918, four prisoners sneaked past the sentries and made their way to the island's shore. Here they fashioned a crude raft of driftwood and planks and cast off for San Francisco. They vanished completely and are presumed to have drowned. Another trio attempted to escape towards San Francisco one night on a driftwood raft. The current carried them out through the Gate that night, and then brought them back in the next morning on the flood tide. Commuters on an early morning ferry spotted them, and by that time the convicts were so cold and seasick that they were delighted to be rescued, even though it meant a return to prison. Sometime later another group left on a raft, this time headed northward towards the Marin shore. Their craft came apart, and by the time they were rescued, the men were clinging to bits and pieces of their raft and one had been numbed unconscious by the cold water.

The Army's rehabilitation program was a remarkable success. The commanding officer could exercise his discretion and return anyone to regular Army duty if he felt the man wanted to make good. An astonishing 70 percent of the soldiers who returned to active duty did, in fact, make good and were credits to their regiments. It was an object lesson in what can be accomplished in rehabilitating minor offenders when the really rotten apples are removed from the barrel.

In 1933 the Army had 225 military prisoners on Alcatraz. Operating costs for its disciplinary barracks were high, however, and the Army looked about for a way to rid itself of the island.

CELLHOUSE, LIGHTHOUSE, AND WARDEN'S HOME IN NOVEMBER OF 1954. This picture was taken from above the southeast end of the island. Angel Island is in the background at the right. (Twelfth Coast Guard District)

FEDERAL PENITENTIARY

The 1930s were the years of the Great Depression. Prohibition was still in effect when the decade began—the "noble experiment" would not be repealed until the end of 1933. With millions of men jobless and desperate, crime was rampant and the nation was terrorized by a wave of organized bootlegging, bank robberies, kidnapings, and murders. The new breed of vicious criminal spawned in the early 1930s was countered by a new breed of law-enforcement agent—the well-publicized G-Man of the Federal Bureau of Investigation (FBI).

The G-Men's success in rounding up gangsters passed on to prison wardens the job of confining them. It wasn't easy. John Dillinger, Public Enemy No. 1, helped ten of his buddies escape from Indiana State Prison, and three of them returned the favor four months later by helping him escape from the Lima City Jail. In June of 1933 a carload of gangsters tried to rescue Frank Nash as he was being returned to prison in Kansas City. In the shoot-out they wounded two FBI agents, killed four officers, and also killed the man they were trying to set free. And so it went. The "mad dogs" simply proved too tough for the ordinary jail. A "super bastille" was needed, and the War Department's desire to abandon Alcatraz released the ideal site. "Hellcatraz" was born.

Alcatraz officially became a federal prison on January 1, 1934. It was to be, as U. S. Attorney General Homer Cummings visualized it, "the ultimate punishment society could inflict upon men short of killing them; the point of no return for multiple losers; the threat [which] harassed or malicious wardens could dangle over unruly charges; the one place in the American penal system that made not even a pretense at rehabilitation, whose one avowed aim was to confine and to punish." A writer summarized the concept more succinctly as "the great garbage can of San Francisco Bay, into which every federal prison dumped its most rotten apples."

The man selected to be warden of the new prison was James A. Johnston, a mild-mannered San Franciscan who had been a successful lawyer, banker, and civic leader. Johnston had previously been warden at both Folsom and San Quentin state prisons, where he earned a reputation as a humanitarian for correcting prison abuses. Many penologists thought Johnston was too "soft" for Alcatraz.

Warden Johnston arrived on The Rock on January 2, 1934 and immediately set about to make the old military prison escape-proof. The soft iron bars on the cell-house windows and most cells were replaced with tool steel, automatic locking devices were installed on cell doors and on the gates that separated the prison into manageable units, canisters were attached to ceilings from which tear gas could be released for mob control, and bars were placed over the sewers and every other outlet. In contrast to the Army's allowing prisoners access to most of the island, the inmates of the federal penitentiary were restricted to the cellhouse and its adjacent recreation yard and to the shops at the north end of the island. All the rest of the island was off-limits to convicts. A 20-foot cyclone fence topped with barbed wire was raised around the entire prison area with gun towers at intervals. More gun towers were placed on the roofs of the buildings and gun boxes on the wall of the exercise yard, all of them connected by catwalks. Guards were specially chosen and trained for their role as keepers of "the human zoo of the world's most dangerous men." Instead of one guard for every ten prisoners, as at other federal prisons, there was one guard for every three prisoners at Alcatraz.

Thirty-two military prisoners remained on Alcatraz and were turned over by the Army to the Justice Department. They had the dubious honor of being numbered one through 32 in Alcatraz's "guest book." Prisoner Number 33 arrived on The Rock on August 2, 1934. His name was Robert Moxon and he was a former soldier who had already served a prison sentence on Alcatraz while it was the Army's disciplinary barracks. He remarked on landing: "Christ, they've sure changed this joint!"

A week later, on August 11th, a group of fourteen convicts arrived from McNeil Island Prison in Washington state. They were the first group of prisoners to be sent from another federal penitentiary. The next shipment was 53 prisoners who arrived on August 22nd from Atlanta, Georgia. By the end of September Alcatraz held 211 prisoners, and by the end of its first year of operation there were 242. The average prisoner count during Alcatraz's 29 years as a federal penitentiary was 263. The highest count was 302 (in 1937) and the lowest was 222 (in 1947).

Warden Johnston kept a tight lid on information about the prison's operation. An unhappy journalist joked that it was easier for a convict to escape from Alcatraz than for a newspaper reporter to get in. In 1938, four years after the prison's opening, Warden Johnston issued one of his rare press releases, which provided the following statistics: The average convict was thirty-five years old and was serving a term of twenty-five years. He read sixty to eighty books and saw four Hollywood movies a year. His favorite movies were musicals, the press release claimed, and his favorite movie star was Shirley Temple.

The vast majority of the convicts were "obscure little thugs who hadn't made a headline in their lives." There were thirty or so "great hoods," such as "Scarface" Al Capone, George "Machine Gun" Kelly, Alvin "Creepy" Karpis, and Arthur "Doc" Barker who had been on the FBI's Public Enemy List of most-wanted criminals. These were the ones that gave The Rock its notoriety.

* *

Alphonse "Scarface" Capone was among the first group of fifty-three convicts transferred from Atlanta prison to Alcatraz in August of 1934. He had risen from the ranks of petty crime to the dominant position in Chicago's underworld. In the 1920s he made the Chicago suburb of Cicero notorious as the headquarters of his speakeasies and gambling enterprises. The U. S. Bureau of

"ARMORER" AT PRISON CONTROL CENTER. Anyone entering or leaving the cellhouse had to pass through three doors controlled jointly by the guard sitting at this position (called the "armorer") and the guard accompanying the visitor. The armorer first scrutinized the visitor through one of the viewing panels of bullet-proof glass and, if satisfied that nothing was amiss, pressed a button that electrically slid back a plate that covered the lock to the first door. The guard with the visitor then unlocked the door with a key he carried, after which the cover plate was slid back. Two more doors (one of solid steel with a vision panel and one of steel bars) had to be passed through in similar fashion. The armorer could communicate by telephone with prison guards in the cellblocks, on the watchtowers, and at numerous points around the island. At frequent intervals the guards had to call the armorer to report the headcount of convicts and to verify that there was no trouble at their posts. An arsenal of submachine guns, high-powered rifles, and other weapons was stored in the area to the left of this photograph. (Golden Gate National Recreation Area)

Internal Revenue estimated the profits from his operations in a single year (1930) as: $10 million from prostitution, $10 million from narcotics, $25 million from gambling, and $50 million from bootlegging. Capone himself pocketed more than $20 million a year. He rode about in a seven-ton armored sedan, and he maintained a suite of fifty rooms in a Chicago hotel that was reached by private elevators and had its own bar, supplied from a cache of liquor in an underground vault. He also had a villa in Florida. For a few years at least the "King of the Underworld" was proving that crime *does* pay.

Capone literally got away with murder until he was tripped up on a charge of carrying a gun and was sentenced to a year in Atlanta prison. This was followed by a ten-year sentence for income tax evasion. With millions in cash stashed away on the outside and many influential allies in political circles, Capone bribed guards for favors so openly that word soon leaked out that he was more in control of the Altanta prison than its warden. The Department of Justice ordered him transferred to Alcatraz.

Capone soon learned that his money could buy no favors on The Rock. The 35-year old convict was registered as "Prisoner Number 85" and was made to follow the same routine as the others. The day began at 6:30 AM with the morning gong. Twenty minutes were allowed for washing, dressing, tidying

LINE OF PRISONERS MARCHING TO INDUSTRIAL SHOPS, ABOUT 1938. The wall of the exercise yard is at the upper right. Prisoners who worked in the shops and laundry at the north end of the island marched there and back to the cellhouse twice a day. Note the guards, watchtowers, and catwalk. (San Francisco Public Library)

up, and taking one's place at the bars of his cell for the first head count of the day. At 6:55 AM the first group of men were released from their cells and marched single file into the mess hall at the northwest end of the cell blocks. They placed food on their trays—typically rolls, dry cereal, milk and coffee—as they filed past the counters. The menu varied and provided a calendar from which cons could tell the day of the week. Twenty minutes were allowed for eating. A whistle blew, the guards checked to see that all the eating utensils were accounted for, and the men marched back to their cells. Then there was another morning head count in the cells, after which the convicts were released in groups for work.

A favorite job was in the bakery, located below the kitchen in the basement of the cellhouse. Here convict bakers managed from time to time to ferment an illicit alcoholic brew, which they made by soaking raisins and other fruit in water and yeast in a covered crock that they would hide under flour sacks. Inevitably someone would celebrate too loudly and a new bakery crew would be assigned. Most of the inmates worked in the shops at the north end of the island. Here some of them worked in the tailor shop to make suits for convicts being discharged or paroled from other prisons. Other inmates were assigned to the rubber mat shop, where they made "bumpers" from old tires for use on Navy ships. Some inmates worked in the furniture factory, shoe repair shop, or the laundry, while still others were assigned to the cleanup, gardening, or some other work detail. (During World War II the tailor shop made field jackets and trousers for the troops, and the mat shop turned out cargo nets for Navy ships. Convict welders repaired buoys used on the antisubmarine net that stretched across the Golden Gate and safeguarded San Francisco.) Capone's first job on The Rock was in the laundry. When word of that leaked out, many soldiers and sailors stationed at facilities around the Bay wrote letters home bragging that the notorious Al Capone was their laundryman.

At 11:30 AM the men returned to their cells and there was another head count. Then the men marched into the mess hall, ate, and marched back to their cells. At noon there was another head count, after which the men were released from their cells to return to their work assignments for the afternoon. At 4:20 PM the men returned again to their cells and there was another head count. At 4:25 PM they marched into the mess hall, ate, and marched back to their cells. At 4:45 PM there was another head count and the final lockup of the day. The doors of their cells would not be opened again until the next morning. There was another check and head count at 8:00 PM, and at 9:30 PM the cell lights were turned off. During the night the guards made three additional head counts of the men in their cells.

At 6:30 AM the next morning the daily routine began again.

On Sundays the routine was varied to allow an hour at chapel in the morning and two hours in the recreation yard in the afternoon (one hour for those who went to chapel). The Sunday routine was followed on Christmas and New Year's Day; all other holidays were completely ignored.

There was some relaxation in later years, but from 1934 to 1940 the grim routine at Alcatraz was made even worse by an enforced rule of silence at all times. Except to request another inmate to pass the salt or sugar during meals,

CONVICT WELDER REPAIRING HARBOR BUOY DURING WORLD WAR II. Work assignments changed shortly after Pearl Harbor. Instead of making prison uniforms and suits for convicts being paroled or discharged, the tailor shop turned out field jackets and trousers for the troops. The rubber mat shop switched from making bumpers to cargo nets for Navy ships. In this photograph an Alcatraz inmate is repairing a buoy of the type used on the net of steel cable that the Navy stretched across the Golden Gate to keep enemy submarines from entering the harbor during World War II. (Golden Gate National Recreation Area)

THE ALCATRAZ LAUNDRY. The original laundry at Alcatraz began operations in November of 1911 in a building alongside the powerhouse at the north end of the island. The laundry was moved in 1940 to the new shop on the northwest side. The laundry at Alcatraz provided service to various Army and Navy posts in the San Francisco Bay area. Here two convicts are pressing towels for the United States Navy. (Golden Gate National Recreation Area)

or to ask for a tool in a prison shop, prisoners were forbidden to talk. Capone was a compulsive talker and chattered away to a fellow con as he walked into the mess hall. He spent the next ten days in solitary in "the dungeon," where the fare was bread and water. As soon as he got out, Capone had to tell others about it and was immediately sent back for another ten days. He was cured of talking for about a week after that, when he was again sent back for ten days. After that the chatter-box clammed up for a long time.

The convicts' isolation from the world was complete. There were no radios or newspapers. Desperate for some word of what was going on outside the prison, Capone offered to pay a guard for a bit of news. The guard reported the bribe to the warden and Capone went back to the dungeon for nineteen days. (Nineteen days was the longest stretch a convict stayed in the dungeon. After that he was removed for a day and given a shower before going back to continue a sentence there.)

Metal detectors were installed at various points that inmates had to pass during the day. These kept the prisoners from carrying tools away from the shops or from hiding metal knives or other weapons. Convicts spoke of them as "snitch boxes." All visitors to The Rock were electronically frisked by one. When Al Capone's mother paid a call, the buzzer sounded as she stepped through the "snitch box." The officer held her purse and she tried again, but the result was the same. The wife of the associate warden was then called and she took Mrs. Capone to a side room, where Mrs. Capone was found to be wearing an old-fashioned, full-length corset with steel ribs. She removed the corset and the "snitch box" let her pass. When she reached the visiting room, she found herself separated from her son by a thick pane of bullet-proof glass. She had to speak through two perforated metal strips set in the base of the window. The tiny holes were offset in the two strips so that no contraband could be passed through. (Telephones were installed a few years later so that prisoners and visitors could converse on opposite sides of the window.) When Mrs. Capone started to speak in her native Italian, the guard insisted she speak in English. In order to be heard by her son on the other side of the window, she had to speak loudly, which made it possible for the guard to monitor the conversation. The entire experience was so upsetting that Mrs. Capone never came back.

Just as the convicts were cut off from the outside world, so did Warden Johnston do everything he could to restrict the public from knowing how the prison operated. When word leaked out that Capone worked in the laundry, the warden reassigned him to mopping the latrines and shower room. There Capone got into a fight with a bank robber named Jimmy Lucas, who stabbed him with a pair of shears and inflicted a slight wound. Capone was in several other fights with inmates, for which both he and his assailants received terms in solitary. Among the other tasks that Capone performed were distributing books from the library to the convicts in their cells and sweeping-up the recreation yard. The once powerful "King of the Underworld" was reduced to a pathetic creature.

After a few years on Alcatraz Capone's mind began to break under the strain. By late 1937 he was a sick and confused man, rumored to be insane. He was transferred to the prison hospital at Alcatraz, where he stayed until January 1939. He was then sent to another federal penitentiary to serve an earlier one-year sentence for contempt of court. In 1940 he was released to his wife, who took him to a walled hideaway in Florida. There he died in 1947 at the age of forty-eight.

* *

George "Machine Gun" Kelly arrived on The Rock in 1934 in the first group of convicts sent there from Leavenworth prison. He was from a prosperous family in Memphis, Tennessee and had a college education. No one knows why he took to bootlegging, but his criminal career was sealed when he met the beautiful Kathryn Shannon, mistress of one Steve Anderson, then the biggest rumrunner in Oklahoma. Kelly was himself a good-looking young man, and he and Kate fell madly in love. They left Anderson's gang and struck out on their own, only for Kelly to be caught and sent to Leavenworth for three years. Kate waited loyally on the outside and they were married when Kelly was released.

Through contacts he had made in Leavenworth, Kelly was soon in touch with the nation's biggets bank bandits. He dropped bootlegging for the more lucrative field of bank robbery and adopted a Thompson submachine gun as his signature weapon.

On July 22, 1933 the Kellys kidnapped an Oklahoma millionaire and collected $200,000 ransom money. Fifty-six days later the FBI men caught up with them in a bungalow apartment in Memphis. Kate was too drunk even to wake up when the agents battered down the door. Kelly reached for his machine gun but thought better when he saw the agents with their itchy fingers. He threw up his arms in surrender and screamed the words that were to give the FBI agents their famous nickname: "It's the government men. Don't shoot, G Men! Don't shoot!"

Kelly was sentenced to life imprisonment and sent to Leavenworth. From there he moved to Alcatraz, where he spent the last twenty years of his life. For all his violent reputation he proved a docile prisoner. Better educated than most, Kelly became a first-class cobbler and furniture-maker, a shop bookkeeper, and somewhat of a Bible expert. He died in Alcatraz on July 17, 1954—his 59th birthday.

* *

Arthur "Doc" Barker was the youngest of a homicidal family reared by "Ma" Barker, a stout, frumpish hillbilly from the Ozarks who had so many paramours that it was uncertain who were the fathers of her four sons. The Barker boys were in and out of jails repeatedly, and it was during one of their incarcerations that they met Alvin Karpis, a cold-eyed six-footer from Montreal whom they nicknamed "Creepy." When they were released, "Creepy" was introduced to "Ma" and the Barker-Karpis partnership was formed.

The Barker-Karpis gang went on a crime spree of bank robberies and murders through Missouri, Kansas, Okalhoma, and Nebrasks. They kidnapped

"Scarface" Al Capone

"Doc" Barker

44

Alvin "Creepy" Karpis

Robert "Birdman
of Alcatraz" Stroud

brewery millionaire William A. Hamm of St. Paul, Minnesota and collected $100,000 ransom money. Their trail was strewn with corpses and Karpis was named Public Enemy No. 1, much to the envy of the Barker boys.

Their crime wave continued and a second kidnapping netted them $200,000 in ransom. The money was marked and provided a trail for the FBI agents. "Doc" Barker was located through one of his girl friends and was caught in a Chicago apartment in January of 1935. "Creepy" Karpis evaded the law for another fifteen months before he was captured in New Orleans. Both arrived at Alcatraz in the fall of 1936.

"Creepy" Karpis belied his size and billing as Public Enemy No. 1 by becoming the most pitiful of the bigshot hoods on The Rock. He was described as "too cowardly to fight and too stupid to keep his mouth shut," and the other inmates took to calling him "The Creep." He unwisely called another inmate a "fink" and was answered with a blow that knocked him unconscious. As soon as he recovered, his assailant knocked him out again. Karpis never struck a blow in retaliation, and his status sank to zero. A short time later "The Creep" was beaten up by a former member of his own gang who, though smaller than his one-time boss, mauled Karpis thoroughly. The other convicts took to shunning him, and Karpis was finally transferred to McNeil Island prison in Washington state. He died there in April of 1962, having spent slightly over twenty-five years behind bars.

"Doc" Barker, though physically small and the least notorious of the big-time hoods, fought a long succession of battles on Alcatraz, both with his fellow cons and with the guards. On the morning of January 13, 1939 he and four other inmates sawed their way out of their cells in the isolation unit, which at that time had bars of soft iron. With an improvised "spreader tool," the gang next forced apart the bars over one window of the cellhouse and vanished into the fog that shrouded the island. When guards discovered their absence, the search began. Searchlights finally picked out the men in one of the island's coves, nearly naked and using their clothes to tie a raft together. The guards shouted for the convicts to stop, but their warning went unheeded and they opened fire. One convict was hit in his legs, and all but "Doc" Barker threw up their hands in surrender. Barker plunged alone into the icy water, but he was hit by several bullets and collapsed. As he was carried back to the prison hospital on a stretcher, with his left leg broken and his skull smashed, he opened his eyes only long enough to groan, "I'm all shot to hell," and died.

* *

"Doc" Barker and his four cohorts were not the first to attempt an escape from the Alcatraz federal prison. The first attempt was made a little more than a year after the prison opened by a 40-year old convict named Joe Bowers, who was serving a 25-year term for robbing a small store of $16.63. Since the local post office happened to be in one corner of the store, Bowers' crime was a federal offense and he ended up at Alcatraz. There he was assigned to burning trash at the incinerator next to a cyclone fence. One morning just after the whistle had signalled the men to return to the cellhouse from their work details, something seemed to snap in Bowers' mind, and he started climbing over the fence. The guard in the south tower yelled for him to stop and fired two warning shots. Bowers continued climbing, and the guard's next shot struck him in the lungs. The convict tumbled headlong from the top of the fence to his death on the jagged shoreline rocks sixty feet below.

During Alcatraz's twenty-nine years as a federal prison, there were a total of fourteen separate escape attempts involving at least thirty-nine inmates. Like Bowers, most of them never got off the island. Only five convicts managed to leave and were never heard from again. They left Alcatraz in two separate escapes that were twenty-five years apart. Though all five are thought to have drowned, no one can say for certain that they did.

The first attempt in which escapees actually managed to get off the island was on December 16, 1937. The two convicts involved were Theodore Cole, a 24-year old kidnapper serving a 50-year term, and Ralph Roe, a 29-year old bank robber serving ninety-nine years. These men had broken out two panes of glass in a waterside window of the industrial building on the northwest end of the island, where they worked in the rubber mat shop. They then sawed through the metal sash to let themselves out, and then used a shop wrench to break the lock on the fence that separated them from the cliff. After a moment's hesitation, they dropped into the icy water below and disappeared. Since the entire Bay area was shrouded in heavy fog that day and there was a swift outgoing tide at the time of their escape, both Cole and Roe are presumed to have drowned.

* *

The bloodiest moments at Alcatraz were in May of 1946, during the three-day "Battle of Alcatraz" between the convicts and their guards. The convicts were led by Joe "Dutch" Cretzer, a bank robber and murderer who had risen to fourth position on FBI Director J. Edgar Hoover's list of Public Enemies. Cretzer had been sentenced to life imprisonment following an escape attempt and the killing of a U. S. Marshall in Washington. He arrived at Alcatraz in the fall of 1940 and made an aborted attempt to escape within a year. Cretzer's two accomplices in the big breakout attempt in 1946 were Bernard Coy, a bank robber, and Marvin Hubbard, a gunman.

The riot began at 1:40 PM on May 2nd, when Coy and Hubbard were the only convicts free in the cellhouse. These two had been assigned to cleaning up the kitchen after lunch and were being searched by Officer Miller, an unarmed guard, before returning to their cells. Coy managed to get behind the guard and, as Miller was searching Hubbard, he knocked the guard down. The nearest armed guard was Officer Burch, who was patrolling the enclosed gun gallery overlooking the cells. Officer Burch was out of sight in the adjacent D Block, where he was investigating a disturbance that had been started at a prearranged signal. In a few moments Coy and Hubbard had kicked Officer Miller unconscious, seized his keys, and released Cretzer and other convicts from their cells.

With a tool improvised from pipes and toilet fixtures, Coy spread apart the bars separating the gun gallery from the cell block and squeezed through the opening. On the gun gallery he managed to surprise and overpower Officer Burch, who was armed with a Springfield rifle and an automatic pistol. With their captured arms Cretzer and Coy then forced the guard in Block D to open the steel door between Block D and the main block of cells. The convicts then entered the Block D area and released the prisoners locked in solitary there.

Other guards were overpowered, and soon the convicts had nine guards held hostage in two cells of the main block. Except for Officer Burch, none of the guards had weapons. Nor did any guard provide the key that was vital to the convicts' escape—the key to the recreation yard, from which the convicts planned to storm the guard towers and walls. Officer Miller had managed to hide the key before being beaten unconscious, and the convicts had been unable to pry the secret from him. Lacking that one key, the prisoners were still prisoners in the cellhouse.

PRISONERS RETURNING FROM WORK IN THE INDUSTRIAL SHOPS. Within the circle is a line of prisoners being marched back from the shops to their cells. The dotted line at the right shows the path taken by "Doc" Barker and his four cohorts in their unsuccessful attempt to escape from Alcatraz (see story in text). (San Francisco Public Library)

48

As the convicts perceived their desperate situation, the prison sirens shrieked a general alarm. In a fit of rage Cretzer fired blindly into the two cells that held the guards. Officer Miller died at once; most of the others were badly wounded, and two pretended to be hit and lay still.

The sirens wailed on. The Coast Guard sent boats to circle the island. All of the off-duty officers and those who lived on the mainland were called back to the island. Sharpshooters with high-powered rifles arrived from military posts. The convicts realized that a counterattack was being organized and that severe retribution would follow. One by one they slipped back into their cells, except for the three leaders. Cretzer, Coy, and Hubbard remained with a rifle, a pistol, and sixty-five rounds of ammunition.

Warden Johnston waited until early evening to attempt to rescue the captured guards. The attempt began with an assault on the west gun gallery. One officer tore open the door, two others fired volleys down the corridor to clear it, and then the team rushed in. They were met by a hail of bullets from the convicts. One guard was killed and three others were wounded. The assault team withdrew and the convicts' firing stopped.

Fourteen volunteers made a second rescue attempt later that night. The officers entered the cellhouse, not sure where the armed convicts might be hiding. In a brief battle, one officer was wounded, but others returned the fire and the remaining officers hauled out the hostages. The dead guard Miller had been kicked and beaten brutally; Officer Corwin's left eye had been shot out by one of Cretzer's bullets; Captain Weinhold had been shot through the chest; Simpson had a torn belly; and Lageson had been shot in the face. All of the wounded guards eventually recovered.

From the moment the hostages were rescued, the prison guards waged war without mercy. Donning masks, they entered the cellhouse and exploded one tear gas bomb after another. They fired at anything that moved outside the cells. Convicts screamed in their cells for mercy, but the three mutineers could not be located. By dawn the white clouds of tear gas made it appear that Alcatraz was on fire. Thousands of San Franciscans thronged to the waterfront to watch the battle. By this time the attackers had decided that Cretzer, Coy, and Hubbard must be hiding in one of the utility corridors that ran between the rows of cells in each cell block and carried the network of electrical conduits and pipes that supplied water, plumbing, and ventilation to the cells on either side.

Warden Johnston determined not to risk any more of his men and mounted an all-out barrage of high-explosive shells that continued through the morning. (Visitors today can see the pock marks from the barrage on the walls inside the D Cell Block.) By Friday afternoon the trio of rebels had been located in the concrete utility tunnel of C Block. Six officers climbed to the roof, where they drilled holes and then dropped grenades and demolition charges into the tunnel. The blasts rocked the building again and again. The three rebels yelled back and retreated further into the tunnel of the utility corridor.

An ear-shattering barrage continued through the night with exploding rifle grenades, demolition bombs, and anti-tank shells. Warden Johnston lifted the siege Saturday morning. Guards then rushed the cellhouse, opened the door to the utility tunnel, and raked the passage with gunfire. They yelled for the rebels inside to surrender, but receiving no answer, they entered the tunnel to dig them out. The guards waded slowly and cautiously through the ankle-deep muck in the tunnel, now a wilderness of broken steam pipes and shattered water lines. At the far end of the tunnel they found the convicts. All three were dead. Coy's body had been ripped by bullets, and Cretzer and Hubbard had bullets through their skulls. Hubbard's body was still warm.

In the trials that followed, two prisoners were sentenced to death for their parts in the death of Officer Miller. Since Alcatraz had no execution facilities of its own, the two were sent to the state prison at San Quentin, where they died in the gas chamber. A third prisoner who participated in the break, an Indian named Clarence "The Choctaw Kid" Carnes who was already serving ninety-nine years for kidnapping, had the death penalty commuted to a second 99-year term because of his youth—he was only nineteen years old at the time of the riot!

* *

Robert F. Stroud (1890-1963), who achieved fame as "the birdman of Alcatraz," was another of the prison's widely known inmates. Stroud had been a young pimp in Juneau, Alaska. A customer beat up his female meal ticket, and Stroud killed him. Since Alaska was then a federal territory, Stroud's crime was a federal offense and he was sentenced (in 1909) to twelve years in the federal prison at McNeil Island. Two years later Stroud injured a fellow inmate and was transferred to Leavenworth. There he stabbed a prison guard to death with an icepick and was sentenced to death. In April of 1920, on the day before he was to hang, President Woodrow Wilson commuted his sentence to life imprisonment. For the next thirty-nine years, first at Leavenworth and then at Alcatraz, Stroud lived in solitary confinement.

It was at Leavenworth that Stroud began studying bird diseases. He bred canaries, assembled a makeshift laboratory, and wrote articles on bird diseases. His publications were widely read by veterinarians, poultrymen, and bird breeders around the country, and they wrote many letters to Stroud asking his advice. In 1942 he published his classic study, *Stroud's Digest of the Diseases of Birds.* The Department of Prisons reacted to Stroud's growing fame. Shortly before Christmas in 1942 Stroud was abruptly transferred to Alcatraz. His birds, books, and hand-made laboratory were all left behind.

When Stroud arrived at Alcatraz in 1942, he was 52 years old and had already spent 33 yers of his life in prison. He was confined in one of the long-term solitary cells of D Block, the section known to Alcatraz cons as "TU," the "treatment unit." Warden Johnston felt some compassion, for he permitted Stoud to receive special bird journals, gave him library privileges, and provided him with enough writing material to continue his correspondence with bird breeders.

Warden Johnston retired in 1948. The new warden was less sympathetic and withheld the special privileges Stroud had enjoyed. Prison rules limiting the number of letters that inmates could receive were invoked, and Stroud was cut off from his public outside. In a further tightening of the screws, Stroud's bird library was confiscated and he was not allowed to keep more than one book in his cell at a time. Stroud filed an appeal with the Federal Court asking that he be allowed to continue his bird studies, but his appeal was denied. His physical and mental health deteriorated, and he entered the prison hospital at Alcatraz. In 1959 Stroud was transferred to the Federal Medical Center at Springfield, Illinois, where he died at the age of seventy-two. The year of his death, 1963, was the year the Alcatraz prison closed.

* *

One of the last escape attempts took place on June 11, 1962, when three convicts disappeared from the island and were never heard from again. The trio's ringleader was Frank Morris, a bank robber and escape artist with an IQ of 135 who had served time in the Louisiana State Prison and the Atlanta Federal Prison. His companions were a pair of brothers, Clarence and John Anglin, who were also doing time for bank robbery. The three convicts used spoons to chip through eight inches of concrete around the ventilating grill of their cells. It was said that such a feat was possible only because of the some-what porous condition of the cellblock structure, which was crumbling in the harsh environment of fog and salt-laden air. Even then the job took months to complete—but time was the one thing the convicts had plenty of.

The three fashioned life-like dummies that they would leave behind to fool the guards into believing they were still in their cells. The dummies had real hair collected from the prison barbership and laboriously glued in place.

When all was finally ready, the three men left their cells one night and crawled into the utility corridor, from which they escaped to the cellhouse roof. Managing to keep out of the sight of guards on the watchtowers, they reached the shore of the island. Here they stopped to inflate a plastic raft they had fashioned from pieces of rain coats, and then paddled off with oars they had made furtively in the machine shop. Since they were never heard from again, and no bodies washed ashore, there is a good chance that they reached shore safely. If they did, they were the first and only convicts to escape successfully from The Rock while it was a federal prison.

* *

A final escape attempt was made on December 12, 1962 by two long-term bank robbers, Paul Scott and Darl Parker. They wriggled through a window in the basement of the cellhouse and made their way to the island's shore. Parker got only a few feet from shore when he was overcome by the cold and the current, and he decided to give up and return. Scott was somewhat sturdier. With the help of a "Mae West" improvised from inflated rubber gloves, he reached San Francisco's shoreline near the south end of the Golden Gate Bridge, about a three-mile swim from Alcatraz. He was close to death from exposure—literally purple from cold—and was unable to pull himself out of the water. Several teenagers spotted Scott at 7:40 AM and phoned the mili-

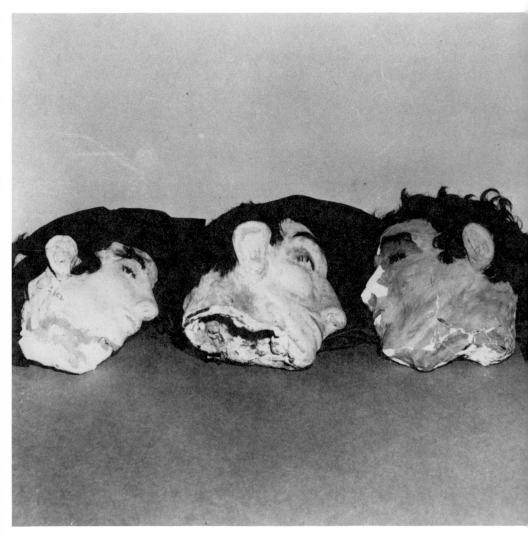

DUMMY HEADS USED IN PRISON ESCAPE IN JUNE 11, 1962. These fake heads were used to fool prison guards into believing that the three escapees were tucked in their beds in their cells. In fact, the convicts had managed to escape through the ventilator ducts of their cells into the utility corridor behind, from which they made their way to cellhouse roof and left the island (see story in text). The ruse provided them with enough time to make their way to the mainland before they were missed. From left to right, the three heads represent Clarence Anglin, John Anglin, and Frank Morris. (Golden Gate National Recreation Area)

CONVICT'S CELL WITH DUMMY IN BED TO DECEIVE GUARDS. This is the cell of one of the three escapees in the breakout of June 11, 1962. (San Francisco Public Library)

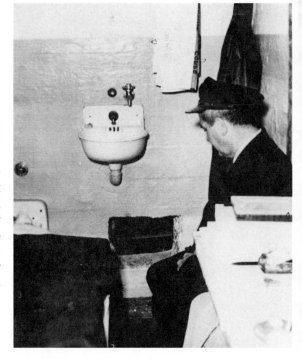

GUARD INSPECTING VENTILATION HOLE THROUGH WHICH THE INMATE OF THIS CELL ESCAPED ON JUNE 11, 1962. The hole is normally covered by an iron grill. The convict removed the grill and then, over a period of months, chipped away at the concrete to make the hole large enough to wriggle through and into the utility corridor behind. (San Francisco Public Library)

tary police at the Presidio that they had found "a body." The MPs saw to it that Scott was shortly back on The Rock.

The two escape attempts in 1962 conspired with other factors to convince the government to close the prison. By then taxpayers were spending several million dollars a year to operate Alcatraz. "At that price," a Congressman complained, "it would be cheaper to give each inmate room and board at the Waldorf Astoria." The cost was simply excessive. It was costing three times as much to maintain a convict at Alcatraz as at any other federal prison. In addition, the physical condition of the prison had so deteriorated that major investments would have been necessary to correct its deficiencies. Finally, the depression-era conditions that had hatched "Hellcatraz" were past and the philosophy of punishment without rehabilitation was discredited.

Attorney General Robert Kennedy flew to San Francisco early in 1963 and held a news conference, at which he announced that the prison would be closed shortly. On March 21, 1963 Alcatraz ceased its operations and the remaining convicts were transferred to other prisons.

* *

In 1964 the Justice Department turned the island over to the General Services Administration (GSA) for disposal as surplus property. One of the first things the GSA did was to spend $20,000 to find out how much it was worth. Bureaucracy's answer: $2,178,000. Of this sum, $2 million was for the buildings, and $178,000 was for the twelve acres for which Fremont had paid $5000 back in 1847.

INDIAN CAMP

California's Indian tribes had for centuries looked upon Alcatraz Island as the dwelling place of evil spirits and had steadfastly shied away from it. Now the descendants of many past generations decided to take a second look at their traditional taboo. In March of 1964, just months after the Justice Department had abandoned Alcatraz, five Sioux Indians landed on the island and staked a claim to it. They argued that under the terms of an 1868 treaty their tribe was given the right to claim federal property that was "not used for specific purpose." They offered to pay the same price that the Federal Government had paid California Indians for lands seized by the whites after the Gold Rush — 47 cents an acre, or $5.64 for the entire island. It was not even close to the value of $2,178,000 that the General Services Administration (GSA) had established.

Then a second set of claimants appeared. Two white men filed a placer mining claim. They identified their claim by a marker on the shore, named it the "Embarassing Mine," and paid a $2.80 filing fee. The Sioux Indians were even less amused than the GSA by this challenge to their claim. They solemnly warned, "Let them remember General Custer." The GSA chose to ignore both claims, and in time both sets of claimants quietly left.

Nothing happened for the next five years. Then the Indians took a third look. On Thanksgiving Day of 1969, a group of over a hundred Indians landed on Alcatraz Island and claimed it for the Indian Nation. They cited the terms of certain Federal treaties which, the Indians argued, gave their tribes the right to repossess abandoned federal property that was within the tribes' original territory.

This time there was no offer of payment. It was a case of outright seizure. Signs appeared to identify the island as Indian property. A spray-painted slogan on the seawall asserted "RED POWER." The Indians proclaimed that they would establish a West Coast Indian Cultural Center and vocational training headquarters on the island. Their main purpose, of course, was to focus national attention on the plight of Indian people. Certainly that purpose was justified, for no minority group has suffered (and continues to suffer) as badly in the United States as the native Americans. Their defiance of the federal government in remaining on the island gained them a good deal of sympathy, despite its illegality and the vandalism they committed.

The GSA chose to ignore the Indians and let their uprising run its course. The same harsh realities that eventually defeated both the Army and the Justice Department must in time convince the Indians of the futility of their occupation of Alcatraz Island. There was no need to force the issue.

Sympathizers on shore sent food and other necessities to the Indians on the island. The Indians obtained electrical power from the transmission lines that operated the lighthouse. The light itself had been automated in November of 1963, so that the station was unmanned when the Indians seized the island. At the end of May 1970 the Coast Guard extinguished the Alcatraz light after more than a hundred years service because "the Indians were blowing fuses like crazy." Lighted buoys were placed at each end of the island as a temporary measure to guide mariners.

A few days later a spectacular midnight fire broke out in an oil shed and destroyed the warden's big house and the living quarters at the base of the lighthouse. On June 8, 1970, the Indians, using a portable rented generator, turned the lighthouse beam back on. It was a symbol of their hope, they said, "that someday the just claims and rightful dignity of the American Indians will be recognized by our fellow citizens."

A year later the Indians bowed to the inevitable, much as their ancestors had been forced to do many years earlier when white men invaded the West, and they withdrew from the island. Federal marshals and Coast Guard cutters helped remove the last of thrm on June 11, 1971. There had been 150 Indians on Alcatraz at the time of the fire; by June of 1971 there were only fifteen (six men, four women, and five children). Their symbolic action to call the attention of the American people to their plight was ended. Their forefathers were right—Alcatraz was a place where only evil spirits could survive.

"INDIAN LANDING." A group of over a hundred Indians landed on Alcatraz Island in 1969 and claimed it for the Indian Nation. This photograph shows the wharf at the southeast end of the island, with the old barracks for enlisted soldiers (later quarters for prison guards and their families) behind the dock. Signs have been painted to identify the island's new "owners." (San Francisco Public Library)

FIRE OF JUNE 1970 DURING INDIAN OCCUPATION. The upper photograph shows smoke from the base of the lighthouse tower; the white building at the left is an apartment for prison guards and their families, and the building in front is a duplex for guards. The lower photograph shows the gutted shell that was once the warden's house, along with the prison cellhouse and the lighthouse tower. (Upper photo courtesy of Twelfth Coast Guard District; lower photo courtesy of the Redwood Empire Association)

INDIANS ISSUING PROCLAMATION BEFORE LEAVING ALCATRAZ.
The Indians ended their eighteen-month occupation of the island in
June of 1971. Before leaving they issued a declaration for the return of
Indian land and unveiled a drawing of their proposed Indian Cultural
Center for the island. Behind them can be seen the smoke-blackened
lighthouse tower and the ruins of the warden's house and the light-
house keeper's quarters. (Golden Gate National Recreation Area)

SOUTH END OF ALCATRAZ ISLAND. This photograph was taken near the end of the Indian occupation in June of 1971. The blackened lighthouse and the charred skeleton of the warden's once beautiful home are at the upper right, with the prison cellhouse behind. The two-story duplex at the south edge of the parade ground was an officer's quarters, built in 1929 on top of the old south battery, where the first cannons had been mounted on Alcatraz Island in 1856. The white buildings on the southwest side of the parade ground (left in the photograph) are apartments erected in 1940 to house prison guards and their families. At the extreme left is the small fog-horn building that replaced the fog bell. Viewers with good eyesight may be able to spot the Indian wigwam near the top of the stairs that climb from the parade ground to the lighthouse area. (Twelfth Coast Guard District)

AERIAL PHOTOGRAPH OF ALCATRAZ ISLAND FROM THE SOUTHEAST. The piles of rubble around the parade ground are all that's left of the apartments and homes for the prison guards and their families, which were demolished for safety prior to the island's opening to the public in 1973. The lighthouse tower is immediately in front of the prison cellhouse; the lightkeeper's quarters were destroyed during the Indian occupation. To the right of the lighthouse is the shell of the warden's home, also destroyed by fire during the Indian occupation. The large builiding to the right (with hip roof and dogleg) was originally a barracks for enlisted soldiers; it was later used to house prison guards. The prison shops, powerhouse, and water tank are in the background. (Twelfth Coast Guard District)

ENJOYING ALCATRAZ TODAY

Alcatraz has always attracted attention. Shortly after it became a federal penitentiary in 1934, telescopes appeared along the waterfront of Fishermen's Wharf and atop Telegraph Hill, and for a nickel or dime a tourist could stare at the grim prison with hopes of spotting a prisoner before the telescope's curtain dropped. Friends of visitors to San Francisco routinely received postcards with a colored photograph of the prison and the inscription, "Having a wonderful time. Wish you were here."

Aside from the convicts, their keepers, and authorized visitors on business, no one was allowed to land on the island. Or even to come close! Signs warned boatmen not to approach nearer than 200 yards and not to anchor within 600 yards. Violators received a warning shot from a high-powered rifle in one of the watchtowers. No boatman ever argued back.

The first steps to open Alcatraz to the public were taken in 1972. In October of that year Congress enacted legislation to create the Golden Gate National Recreation Area (GGNRA). GGNRA was to be the first of the "new look" of city-linked national parks, with over 34,000 acres that included the northern waterfront of San Francisco, Fort Point, Fort Mason, Aquatic Park, Baker Beach, Phelan Beach, Lands End, the Cliff House area, Ocean Beach, Fort Funston, the Marin Headlands, and other nearby areas, as well as Alcatraz Island. Congress' act was quickly signed into law by President Richard Nixon, who was then completing his first term and campaigning for a second.

A year elapsed between the time GGNRA was created and the ruins from the Indians' vandalism could be removed and the buildings made safe for visitors. On October 25, 1973 Alcatraz was officially opened to the public, and it quickly became the most popular part of the GGNRA. It's an interesting fact that Alcatraz attracts more visitors now in a single day than all the convicts held there during its twenty-nine years as a federal prison. The total number of prisoners was a little over 1000, and the average number of daily visitors is close to 1500.

Today's visitors reach Alcatraz by a 15-minute ride aboard one of the ferries operated by Harbor Tours. The ferries leave from Pier 43 of San Francisco's Embarcadero. The first one leaves each morning at 9:00 AM; thereafter, ferries leave every 45 minutes. During the summer season (May to September), the last ferry leaves from Pier 43 at 5:15 PM; during the rest of the year, at 3:00 PM. Tickets are sold at the dock, but as the boat is usually filled, reservations are recommended to avoid disappointment. Tickets can be reserved by calling Harbor Tours at 546-2805 or by writing to them at Pier 41, San Francisco, California 94133. Allow an advance of one month for summer sailings, and two weeks for sailings from October to April. Round-trip fare is $2.50 for

ALCATRAZ ISLAND FROM THE WEST. The prison cellhouse dominates this scene from its position on the island's upper plateau. The recreation or exercise yard is the enclosure to the left of the cellhouse. At the one corner of the exercise yard is the water storage tank. The two buildings near the edge of the island at the northwest end (left foreground in the photograph) are the industrial shops, where convicts made furniture, rubber mats, and clothing and operated a laundry that served military posts around the San Francisco Bay. Behind the shops is the powerhouse, identified by its tall smokestack. The leveled area at the southeast end of the island (right in the photograph) is the old Army parade grounds; the piles of rubble around it are the ruins of residences for prison guards and their families. Overlooking the parade ground is the lighthouse tower, with the ruins of the warden's home just behind. The small box-like buildings at opposite tips of the island house fog horns. (Golden Gate National Recreation Area)

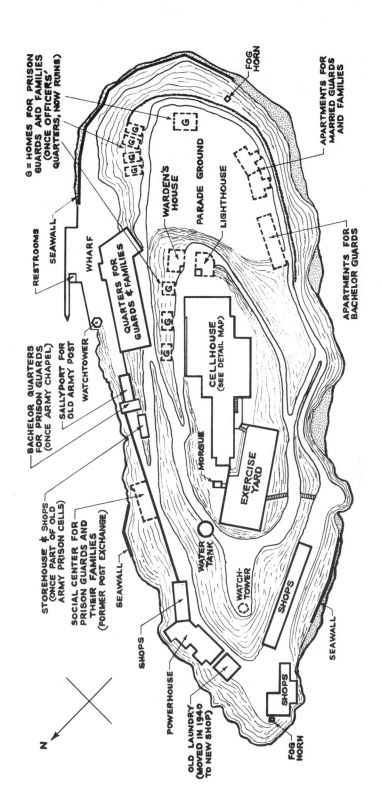

Visitor's Map of Alcatraz

G = HOMES FOR PRISON GUARDS AND FAMILIES (ONCE OFFICERS' QUARTERS, NOW RUINS)

FOG HORN

APARTMENTS FOR MARRIED GUARDS AND FAMILIES

WARDEN'S HOUSE

PARADE GROUND

LIGHTHOUSE

APARTMENTS FOR BACHELOR GUARDS

RESTROOMS

SEAWALL

WHARF

QUARTERS FOR GUARDS & FAMILIES

WATCHTOWER

CELLHOUSE (SEE DETAIL MAP)

MORGUE

EXERCISE YARD

BACHELOR QUARTERS FOR PRISON GUARDS (ONCE ARMY CHAPEL)

SALLYPORT FOR OLD ARMY POST

STOREHOUSE & SHOPS (ONCE PART OF OLD ARMY PRISON CELLS)

SOCIAL CENTER FOR PRISON GUARDS AND THEIR FAMILIES (FORMER POST EXCHANGE)

SEAWALL

SHOPS

WATER TANK

WATCH-TOWER

SHOPS

POWERHOUSE

OLD LAUNDRY (MOVED IN 1940 TO NEW SHOP)

SHOPS

FOG HORN

SEAWALL

N

adults and teenagers, $1.25 for children from 5 to 11 years of age, and is free for those under five. (Costs are as of March 1981.) The fare includes a 1½-hour guided tour led by a park ranger.

* *

Your tour of Alcatraz starts at the wharf on the southeast side of the island, where the boats are met by rangers of the National Park Service. One of the island's vital statistics that's worth noting before setting out on the 1½-hour tour is that there are about 400 toilets on the island, including those in the convicts' cells, but almost none of them work! The only toilets in working condition on the entire island are located in the restrooms near the dock. Your guide will wait.

The large concrete-block building overlooking the dock area was a military barracks for enlisted Army men, begun in 1865 and finished in 1905. From 1934 to 1963 it provided living quarters for married guards of the federal penitentiary. Today it houses a small museum and bookstore that can be visited at the end of the tour. Also overlooking the dock area is a watchtower dating from the island's years as a federal penitentiary.

Visitors walk from the dock area up a switchback road that winds up the hill. A short distance beyond the dock is the old guardhouse and the fortified entrance to the military post. One enters through the old sallyport, which was constructed to allow troops to rush out or "sally forth" from the fort against an enemy. Enemy forces were prevented from entering by heavy gates at each end of the long passageway of the sallyport. The walls of the sallyport are thick and are pierced with rifle slits to allow soldiers to fire at the invaders that never came.

Beyond the first bend of the switchback road, enjoying a view of Angel Island and the communities of the East Bay, are the ruins of the old post exchange. This building was once the social center for prison guards and their families, where they bowled, danced, played cards, and enjoyed themselves. The gardens along the roadway grow in soil brought from the mainland when Alcatraz was an Army post. The gardens were once beautifully maintained by the military prisoners and later by the prison guards and their families. They are now untended and the flowers are mixed with weeds, but there are still colorful displays of geraniums, pelargonia, nasturtiums, honeysuckle, poppies, daisies, ice plant, and other flowers in season. The plants survive on their own, receiving water only from the fog and winter rains.

The walk up the ramp next passes the military chapel and infirmary, built over the guardhouse and sallyport. The use of the chapel for religious services was discontinued when Alcatraz became a federal prison, as it was too risky to allow convicts out of the cellhouse area. The chapel became a residence for bachelor guards during the federal prison years (1934 to 1963).

At the top of the road are the ruins of the warden's house. Built after the turn of the century for the Commandant of the Army's prison, it had eighteen rooms, hardwood floors, and all the amenities of an upper middle class home.

This once beautiful home, built in the Mission Revival style, was destroyed in 1971 during the Indian occupation. Across from the warden's house is the lighthouse which was built in 1909 to replace the earlier one of 1854. The lighthouse tower is intact and still operates as an unmanned unit, but the keeper's quarters at its base were destroyed along with the warden's house.

To the south the warden's house and the lighthouse overlook a flat paved area that was leveled in 1875 to provide a parade ground. This area was the main living compound on the island for guards and their families during the federal penitentiary years. Most of the prison staff lived on the mainland and commuted to work by boat, but about a third lived on the island. Between fifty and sixty families lived on the island with over a hundred children ranging from infants to teenagers. They and the bachelor guards lived in three multi-story apartment buildings on the southwest side of the parade ground and in remodeled Army officers' homes on the south and southeast. The enlisted men's barracks was also remodeled into quarters for guards and their families, and the chapel was converted into quarters for bachelor guards. Children used the parade ground as their private playground and fished from the island's edge. Besides going back and forth to school by boat, their lives differed from those of most children in two important limitations: First, because the island is small, they were not allowed to keep cats or dogs as pets. And second, they were not allowed to play with toy guns, cap pistols, or rubber daggers. Their mothers, of course, never had their doorbells rung by the Fuller Brush Man or the Avon Lady.

The guards' homes and apartments were razed at the time GGNRA assumed responsibility for the island, since they were unsafe for visiting. The piles of rubble that remain will be removed at some future time, and plans are to dig up the concrete pavement and reconstruct the old Army fortifications built back in the 1850s on the south end of the island. The GGNRA also hopes to landscape this area and provide tables for picnics.

To the north of the warden's house and the lighthouse one enters the second floor of the prison cellhouse. This huge, three-story warehouse-like building was constructed by military prisoners in 1909-1912, while the Army operated Alcatraz as "The Pacific Branch of the United States Military Prison." It is built over the foundations of the old citadel built by the Army back in the 1850s.

The prison's administrative offices were located across the front of the second floor. To enter the prison cell block area from the front of the building, one had to pass through a succession of three interlocked security barriers: the first a barred gate, the second a solid steel door with an eye-level slit, and the third another barred gate.

One's first impression on entering the cell blocks is that of an immense aviary, lined with a multitude of bird cages. The cells are grouped in four "blocks," labeled simply A, B, C, and D. Block A, on the east side, is one of the smaller blocks. It had been used for holding military prisoners in solitary confinement, and its use as the "isolation unit" continued after the Justice Department took over the island in 1934. The cell doors in Block A still have their

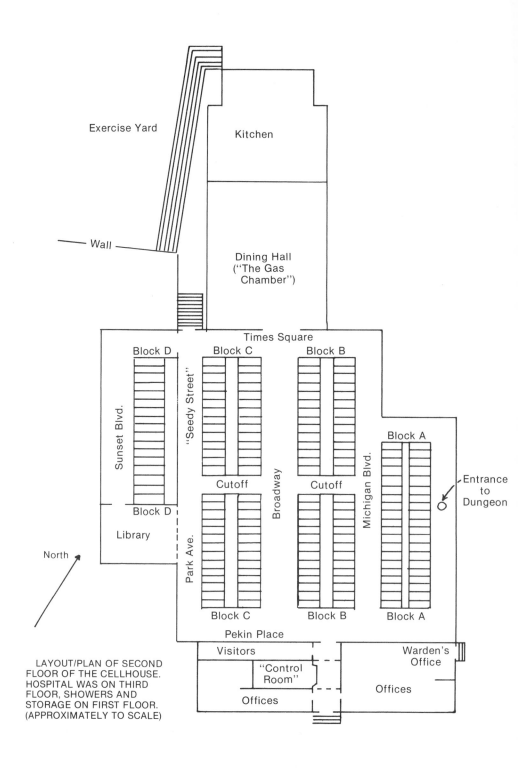

Exercise Yard

Kitchen

Wall

Dining Hall
("The Gas
Chamber")

Times Square

Block D

Block C

Block B

"Seedy Street"

Sunset Blvd.

Broadway

Michigan Blvd.

Block A

Entrance
to
Dungeon

Cutoff

Cutoff

Block D

Library

Park Ave.

North

Block C

Block B

Block A

Pekin Place

Visitors

Warden's
Office

LAYOUT/PLAN OF SECOND
FLOOR OF THE CELLHOUSE.
HOSPITAL WAS ON THIRD
FLOOR, SHOWERS AND
STORAGE ON FIRST FLOOR.
(APPROXIMATELY TO SCALE)

"Control
Room"

Offices

Offices

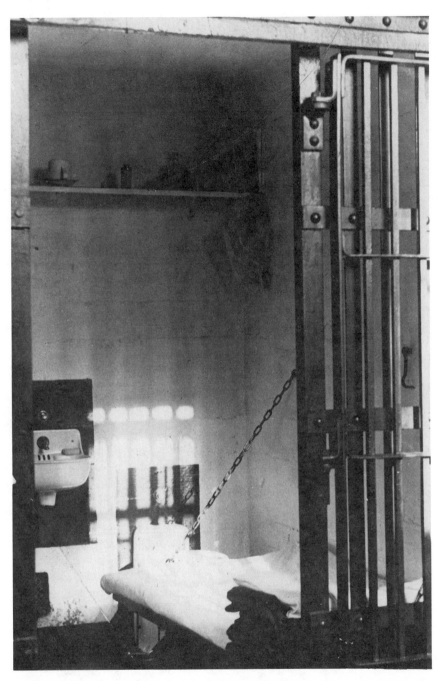

CONVICT CELL IN BLOCK A. This is the original type of cell built in 1909-1912, when the cellhouse was constructed to hold military prisoners. The doors had bars and straps of soft iron and swung out-wards on hinges. (Golden Gate National Recreation Area)

original bars and straps of soft iron from the military period; in the other three cell blocks, the bars are of hardened tool steel. In 1940, the year after five convicts broke out of their cells in Block A, the modernization of Block D was completed, and Block D then became the isolation unit for holding convicts in solitary confinement, of which more later. After that, Block A was used for storing materials rather than prisoners. But a reminder of its first years remain in the hole in the floor that is the entrance to the notorious "dungeon," a dank dark hole down in the building's foundations. Prisoners who were especially troublesome were sent to the dungeon, where they were chained to the wall and subsisted on bread and water.

The two center blocks, Blocks B and C, were the main confinement area. Most of the prison traffic moved along the wide aisle between these two cell blocks, which the convicts named "Broadway." The narrower outer aisles were named "Michigan Boulevard" (between A and B Blocks) and "Seedy Street" (between C and D Blocks). The cross-aisle that ran across the cellhouse at the front end of the building was called "Pekin Place." At one side of "Pekin Place" was the visitors' room, which had four cubicles with small windows through which outsiders had their only opportunity to "peek into" the prison. At the opposite end of the cell blocks was a large, wall-mounted clock, and the cross aisle there was known as "Times Square."

Blocks B and C were each 150 feet long and were divided into two sections by a 10-foot wide space called "The Cutoff," which ran at right angles to the main aisles. The blocks were split lengthwise by narrow utility corridors that carried the electrical conduits, ventilation ducts, and pipes for supplying water and plumbing to the cells on either side. The utility corridors were referred to by cons as "the tunnels." They were closed by solid steel doors at either end on all tiers and were inaccessible to the convicts.

The total number of cells in Blocks B and C is 336, arranged as follows: Each block has two banks of cells separated by the utility corridor. Each bank has three tiers of cells, one over the other. Each tier has a row of 28 cells alongside each other. (If you're a mathematician, the combined total of 336 cells for the two cell blocks can be figured out this way: Twenty-eight cells in each tier times three tiers in a bank equals 84 cells in each bank; multiply the 84 cells in each bank by two banks, one on either side of the utility corridor, to get 168 cells in each cell block; then, for the two cell blocks there would be twice 168 cells, or a total of 336 cells. Got it?) Since each convict had his own cell (an arrangement to discourage homosexual activity), the prison's capacity was 336 inmates. However, the most the prison ever held at any one time was 302 convicts, and it usually held around 270.

The cells in Blocks B and C measure 5 feet wide by 9 feet long. Their end walls are concrete, their side walls are solid steel, and their fronts are sliding doors of steel bars. They contained a cot, a wash basin, a toilet without a lid or seat, and a table and chair. There was a shelf for personal belongings on one wall. These cramped quarters were "home" to the average prisoner for fourteen to fifteen hours a day, and for eight to ten years. When the GGNRA rangers first started guiding tours through the cell blocks at Alcatraz, visitors were per-

"BROADWAY." This is the main aisle through the cellhouse, between Blocks B and C. The Ranger is explaining the cells and the locking mechanism to the visitors. This view looks toward the front of the cellhouse, with the gun gallery barely visible at the far end of "Broadway." (Golden Gate National Recreation Area)

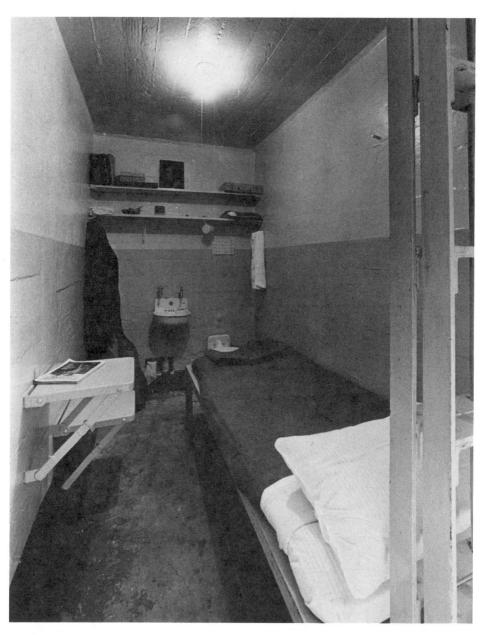

CELL IN THE MAIN CELL BLOCK OF THE FEDERAL PENITENTIARY.
When the Justice Department took over the military prison from the
Army in 1934, they upgraded the facilities to improve security. One of
their changes was to replace the old cell doors in Blocks B and C with
new doors that had bars of hardened tool steel instead of soft iron, and
that slid open and close in front of the cell opening instead of pivoting
outwards on hinges. (Golden Gate National Recreation Area)

mitted to enter the cells for a close look, and the rangers would slam the doors shut and lock them in to add realism to their experience. There were no problems for the first years, but one day the mechanism jammed with several prisoners (sorry, visitors) locked inside the cells. They were trapped for 4½ hours before a locksmith could be brought to unjam the door locks and release them. Since then, visitors must use their imaginations to sense the feeling of confinement that oppressed the convicts.

The fourth cell block, Block D, was the isolation unit. Convicts referred to it as the "TU," or "treatment unit." It has only one row of cells and is separated from Blocks B and C by concrete walls and a solid steel door. Since it is on the west side of the building, with tall windows facing towards the Golden Gate, convicts dubbed the aisle in front of these cells "Sunset Boulevard."

The cells in Block D are larger than in Blocks B and C. Convicts held in solitary were not allowed to leave their cells, even for meals; instead, they were provided with "room service." They ate the same food as the other prisoners, but their meals were pureed in a blender and then thinned with beet juice and served to them in paper cups. This removed their access to dishes and flatware. Once a week each convict was taken alone from the "treatment unit" for an hour of solitary exercise in the recreation yard and for a solitary shower.

There are three types of cells in Block D. The cells on the first level with barred doors were for the "short termers," which meant anyone serving from a day to a year in solitary for minor offenses against prison rules. The cells on the second and third levels, all with barred doors, were for the "long termers," or those serving a year or longer in solitary for serious offenses, such as assaulting another prisoner. Robert Stroud, "the Birdman of Alcatraz," was one of the long-termers in solitary; he occupied different cells at various times during the seventeen years he was at Alcatraz, all of them in solitary. Including the time in solitary in Leavenworth prison before coming to Alcatraz, Stroud spent an incredible forty years of his life in solitary confinement, a record unequalled by any other prisoner anywhere!

The third type of cell in Block D is on the lower level and has two doors, an inner one that is barred and an outer one of solid steel. Once the outer doors are shut, these cells are completely dark and nearby sounds are muffled, so that prisoners are totally isolated. Cell Number 14 at the far end was reserved for the most rebellious prisoners. It was called "The Hole," and it contained nothing more than a small hole in the floor for the prisoner's elimination. There was not a mattress, sink, or toilet in "The Hole," and if the prisoner remained rebellious, he was left there without clothing. The floors of "The Hole" and the other five cells are of thick steel, which is a good conductor of heat. When a naked convict sat or lay on the floor, a large part of his body was in contact with the cold metal, which continually sucked the heat away from his body. One survived by standing or by resting on one's knees and elbows or hands.

If you're game, your guide will let you enter one of the six cells and close the solid door so that you can experience what it was like to be isolated in the dark. Some kids think it's "neat." The author once shared one of these cells for a few seconds with another "guest" who had brought his accordion along for an

CONVICT IN CELL. Musical instruments, such as the guitar being played by this inmate, could be purchased with funds earned by working in the laundry or shops at Alcatraz. Convicts were paid as little as seven cents an hour for the lowest-paid jobs in the 1960s. Aside from providing an opportunity to earn money for prison luxuries, the jobs provided relief from the grinding monotony of the prison routine. (Golden Gate National Recreation Area)

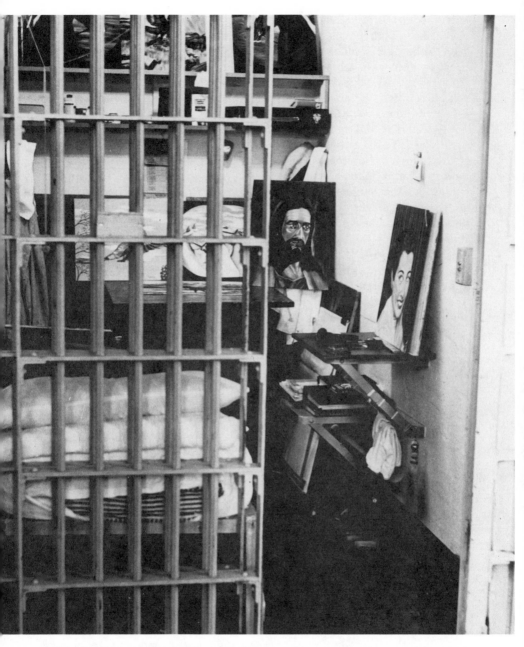

CELL WITH AN INMATE'S ART WORK. More than thirty convicts pursued art as a hobby at one time. This photograph, taken in March of 1956, shows several paintings displayed in the artist's cell. The prisoners paid for their own materials with money they earned by working in the laundry or one of the prison's shops for making furniture, rubber mats, clothing, etc. (San Francisco Public Library)

impromptu concert. He said he only wanted to try out the cell's acoustics. I was glad he hadn't brought bagpipes!

Within each cellblock a single guard patrolled the floor constantly, unarmed except for a billy club. Above him, armed guards watched from the "gun gallery," a walkway enclosed by bars and heavy wire that overlooked the cell block area. The armed guards were themselves locked in the gun gallery for their 8-hour watches.

Alcatraz served up two nice surprises for inmates—hot showers and "four star" food. The day's three meals were served in the mess hall at the north end of the cellhouse. From its opening in 1934, Warden Johnston insisted that the food at Alcatraz be the best at any federal prison, and it was. Government regulations set a minimum of 2100 calories per day for each inmate, but the convicts at Alcatraz averaged 3100 to 3600 calories per day and some gained forty pounds during their stretches. Prisoners could take as much food as they wanted, but they had to eat everything they took and leave clean plates or they would miss meals the next day. Each man was responsible for his own eating utensils and had to turn them in at the end of each meal. "Misplacing" one's knife or fork invited a visit to the "treatment unit."

When several hundred convicts assembled there for meals, the mess hall was the most dangerous place in the prison. A guard armed with a submachine gun patrolled along a catwalk outside the windows on the west side. Another armed guard sat in a gun cage midway along the wall. For added safety, canisters of tear gas were mounted on the ceiling for quick release in case of a riot. The presence of the gas canisters caused the convicts to christen their dining room "The Gas Chamber."

Warden Johnston's philosophy in providing good food was more than just to "keep 'em happy." Ample amounts of food together with restricted exercise was one way of keeping the convicts too "soft" for swimming off the island. For the same reason, there were no cold showers. Prisoners showered in hot water so that they could not condition their bodies to survive in the icy waters of the Bay.

At the opposite end of Block D from the mess hall was the prison library. With time on their hands, convicts read much more than the average person. The typical inmate read between sixty and eighty books a year. Law books were a predictable favorite, as were also books on philosophy and texts for mathematics and physics. In later years the University of California provided extension courses. Some convicts became expert lawyers and prepared numerous appeals, both for themselves and other inmates. Books with sex and violence were not carried in the library. Neither were tide tables.

The group of cells in Block C that faced the library were favored by the cons, since they did not face other cells across the aisle and therefore provided some small privacy. These cells also enjoyed somewhat restricted views of San Francisco through the library windows in the opposite wall. The cons dubbed these choice quarters "Park Avenue."

Outside the cellhouse is the exercise yard, enclosed on three sides by high walls and on the other by the cellhouse. On Sundays the prisoners were allowed into the exercise yard for two hours. They could play basketball, softball, shuf-

CELLHOUSE AND SOUTHEAST CORNER OF EXERCISE YARD. At the left side of this photograph is the mess hall and kitchen. Note the gun cage alongside the wall, from which an armed guard kept watch through the windows while the prisoners ate their meals. This gun cage connected by a catwalk to a watchtower beyond the right side of the photograph. A net for playing volleyball is in the left foreground, in the exercise yard. The section of the cellhouse in the back is one end of the solitary unit, Block D. (San Francisco Public Library)

TWO VIEWS OF THE EXERCISE OR RECREATION YARD. In the upper view, a baseball game is in progress at the north end of the yard. The dark rectangle on the wall near first base is a door which opens to a walkway that leads to the laundry and shops. (Golden Gate National Recreation Area, both photos)

RECREATION YARD, FROM WITHIN AND WITHOUT. In the upper photograph, two unarmed guards stand at the right of the groups of prisoners huddled together in the warm sunshine. The lower photograh shows a guard armed with an automatic rifle watching from the walk along the top of the wall. (Golden Gate National Recreation Area, both photos)

fleboard, or just relax as they chose. Some were joggers. Softball on Alcatraz had its special rules; batting the ball over the walls, for example, was an automatic out rather than a homerun. A favorite spot for relaxing was at the top of the stairs next to the cellhouse, since one could look over the wall from this spot towards San Francisco and the outside world. Armed guards patrolled the exercise yard on the catwalks and the fenced walkways atop the walls, and several unarmed guards walked about the yard.

Overlooking the exercise yard to the north is the water tower. It held 250,000 gallons of fresh water and was refilled every few days by barges from San Francisco. The high cost of water was a major operating expense for the prison.

Beyond the door at the west side of the exercise yard is the walkway to the shops, where prisoners made gloves, brushes, furniture, clothing, or boat bumpers and operated a laundry for military bases in the Bay area. Work was not mandatory, but most prisoners did in order to send money to their families, to accumulate savings for their release, or simply to offset the deadly routine of being locked in a cell. Their wages varied from as little as seven cents an hour, depending upon the type of work done. Tailors were the highest paid and received on the order of twenty-five to thirty cents an hour.

* *

The entire trip today, from San Francisco's Embarcadero to the island and back to San Francisco, takes about two hours—two 15-minute boat rides there and back, and a 1½-hour guided tour on the island. The walk is only about one and a half miles long, but there are steep climbs uphill from the dock and other points, there are some stairs, and there are some uneven walkways, all of which make the walk seem much longer. Comfortable walking shoes should be worn. Also, since the island is exposed to cold ocean winds and damp fog, warm clothing is generally advisable, even when it's sunny and warm on the mainland.

Finally, a hat with a broad brim is suggested in summertime for the walk on the west side of the island (optional), where sea gulls are numerous. The birds are the island's last "cannoneers," and their droppings are released without regard for any sightseers below. Now and then someone is hit. Funny thing about those damn birds—they seem to think the island still belongs to them.

CONVICTS RETURNING FROM WORK IN THE PRISON SHOPS. At the foot of the stairs the cons must pass through a "snitch box" that electronically frisks them for any hidden metal objects, such as knives or shop tools. At the left are the two industrial shop buildings at the north end of the island (the nearer one built in 1940 and the other built in 1929). At the top of the stairs is the wall of the recreation yard. Note the catwalk connecting the north watchtower to the roof of the farther shop, and the gun boxes for the guards at the corners of the recreation yard wall and on the roof of the shop. (Golden Gate National Recreation Area)

"NEW INDUSTRIES BUILDING." Construction of this building began in 1939 at the northwest end of Alcatraz Island, just south of the older prison shop. When completed the following year, the main floor housed a clothing factory, dry-cleaning plant, furniture factory, brush factory, and an office. The second floor housed the laundry, which previously had been located in the complex of buildings with the powerhouse. This building was 300 feet long and cost $186,000. The prison cellhouse and the walls of the recreation yard are above, wtih a gun box at the corner and a watchtower to the right. The top of the lighthouse can barely be seen above the cellhouse. (Golden Gate National Recreation Area)

NORTHWEST END OF ALCATRAZ ISLAND. The lighthouse tower barely protrudes above the prison cellhouse at the top center. This photograph shows the watchtower and catwalks from which armed guards patrolled the shop area where convicts worked. The large storage tank has a capacity of 250,000 gallons of fresh water and was refilled every few days by a barge from San Francisco. The building at the left with the tall chimney is the powerhouse which supplied steam and electricity to the prison. The small gabled building in front of the shop (just above the stern of the boat) houses a fog bell. (Redwood Empire Association)

EPILOGUE

Besides the Spanish name "Isla de Alcatraces" and its Americanized version "Alcatraz Island," and besides the informal names "Bird Island," "White Island," "The Battleship in the Bay," "The Rock," "Hellcatraz," and "Indian Landing," the island had still one other name. It was a name given by the Russians, who had moved down the Pacific Coast from Alaska in pursuit of fur-bearing sea otters and had come to California and to San Francisco Bay in the late 1700s. It appears on a Russian map of 1823 and was probably occasioned by the hazards that the island presented to sailors. Of all the names, it seems the one that best summarizes the island's history.

The Russian name? "ZABELIAKA OSTROV," or "Troublemaker Island."

NOTES AND REFERENCES

DISCOVERY AND NAMING

The effectiveness of Alcatraz Island for obscuring the opening through the Golden Gate and delaying the discovery of San Francisco Bay by early explorers is analyzed in an article, "The Delayed Discovery of San Francisco Bay," by H. F. Raup (*California Historical Society Quarterly*, vol. 27, pp. 289-296, 1948).

A detailed discussion of the Spanish explorations that resulted in the discovery of San Francisco Bay can be found in the book, *San Francico Bay: Discovery and Colonization*, by Theodore Treutlein (San Francisco, 1968). Professor Treutlein's book gives a very complete retelling of the expeditions of Portola (1769) and DeAnza (1775-76) that resulted in the discovery and settlement of San Francisco.

Information on the naming of Alcatraz Island is from *California Place Names: The Origin and Etymology of Current Geographical Names*, by Erwin G. Gudde (University of California Press, Berkeley, 2nd edition, 1969).

The quotation on the number of pelicans on Alcatraz Island is from an article, "Duhaut-Cilly's Account of California in the Years 1827-1828," translated from the French by Charles F. Carter (*California Historical Society Quarterly*, vol. 8, pp. 239-245, 1929).

THE BATTLESHIP IN THE BAY

Land grants made during the years when California was part of Mexico were confused by poor descriptions, incomplete records, and many forged documents. It took many years to settle the claims, and in the end, the lawyers were the principal beneficiaries of the protracted litigations. Historians give several versions of what happened in the case of Alcatraz Island. Those interested in the details can find one recounting at pages 5 through 9 of Erwin B. Thompson's comprehensive study, *The Rock: A History of Alcatraz Island, 1847-1972* (National Park Service, Denver, Colorado, 1979). Thompson's book is also the chief source of information on the fortifications constructed and the armament mounted during this period (pp. 10-110).

The unsuccessful plot of Asbury Harpending and his fellow southern sympathizers to capture California for the Confederacy is part of San Francisco's fascinating history and is recounted with more or less detail in various histories of the city. Excellent short accounts are given in the booklet by J. G. Motheral, *Fort Point: "Gibraltar of the Pacific"* (Fort Point Museum Association, San Francisco, 1971) and as Chapter 2, "The Rebel" in the book by John Godwin, *Alcatraz: 1868-1963* (Doubleday & Company, New York, 1963; reprinted in paperback by Pocket Books, Inc., New York, 1964).

Additional information on the fortifications about the Bay during this period can be found in the article "San Francisco Harbor Defenses During the Civil War" by Benjamin F. Gilbert (*California Historical Society Quarterly*, vol. 33, pp. 229-240, 1954).

The quotation from (then) Lieutenant McPherson's letter is from an article, "California Letters of Major-General James McPherson, 1858-1860," by William F. Strobridge (*Ohio History*, Ohio Historical Society, volume 81, number 1, winter 1972).

FIRST LIGHTHOUSE ON THE WEST COAST and NEW LIGHTHOUSE

The primary source of information for these two sections is the excellent and readable book by Ralph C. Shanks, Jr. and Janetta Thompson Shanks, *Lighthouses of San Francisco Bay* (Costano Books, San Anselmo, California, 1976; pp. 14-21).

COMBINATION FORT AND MILITARY PRISON

The primary source of information in this section is again Erwin N. Thompson's comprehensive study, *The Rock: A History of Alcatraz Island, 1847-1972* (National Park Service, Denver, Colorado, 1979).

The quotation from the soldier in the Philippines is part of a letter from Howard Middleton written on October 21, 1898 to his mother and is reproduced in an article, "California Soldiers in the Philippines," edited by Harold F. Taggart (*California Historical Society Quarterly*, vol. 31, pp. 49-67, 1952).

The account of the four clever prisoners who escaped with forged pardons is based on the account in John Godwin's book, *Alcatraz: 1868-1963* (Doubleday & Company, New York, 1963; reprinted in paperback by Pocket Books, Inc., New York, 1964; pp. 10-12).

The historian's evaluation of the great sham battle of July 4, 1876 is that of B. E. Lloyd, from his book *Lights and Shades in San Francisco* (A. L. Bancroft and Co., San Francisco, 1876).

MILITARY PRISON AND DISCIPLINARY BARRACKS

The primary source of information in this section is again Erwin N. Thompson's comprehensive study, *The Rock: A History of Alcatraz Island, 1847-1972* (National Park Service, Denver, Colorado, 1979). The list of prison rules and regulations is slightly abridged from the list given by Thompson at pp. 332-333. The quotation of the Army's Judge Advocate General in 1913 is from pp. 245-246.

FEDERAL PENITENTIARY

Information for this section was obtained principally from the following three books: (1) John Godwin, *Alcatraz: 1868-1963* (Doubleday & Company, New York, 1963; republished in paperback by Pocket Books, Inc., New York, 1964); (2) J. Campbell Bruce, *Escape from Alcatraz* (McGraw-Hill Book Co., New York, revised edition, 1974; reprinted in paperback by Comstock Editions, Sausalito, California, no date); and (3) Erwin N. Thompson, *The Rock: A History of Alcatraz Island, 1847-1972* (National Park Service, Denver, Colorado, 1979). The brief accounts of the careers of Al Capone and other convicts held at Alcatraz, as well as the account of the prison riot of 1946, have been condensed from the accounts given in these three books.

For additional details on the prison riot of 1946, read the excellent book by Don DeNevi and Philip Bergen, *Alcatraz '46: The Anatomy of a Classic Prison Tragedy* (Leswing Press, San Rafael, California, 1974).